Debt Free Blueprint
Learn Strategies To Get Out Of Debt Fast, Pay Off Mortgages, Credit Card And Money Management Skills

AF706519

© Copyright 2021 Jake Robbins- All rights reserved.

In no way is it legal to reproduce, duplicate, or transmit any part of this document in either electronic means or in printed format. Recording of this publication is strictly prohibited and any storage of this document is not allowed unless with written permission from the publisher. All rights reserved.

The information provided herein is stated to be truthful and consistent, in that any liability, in terms of inattention or otherwise, by any usage or abuse of any policies, processes, or directions contained within is the solitary and utter responsibility of the recipient reader. Under no circumstances will any legal re- sponsibility or blame be held against the publisher for any reparation, damages, or monetary loss due to the information herein, either directly or indirectly.

Respective authors own all copyrights not held by the publisher.

Legal Notice:

This book is copyright protected. This is only for personal use. You cannot amend, distribute, sell, use, quote or paraphrase any part or the content within this book without the consent of the author or copyright owner. Legal action will be pursued if this is breached.

Disclaimer Notice:

Please note the information contained within this document is for educational and entertainment purposes only. Every attempt has been made to provide accurate, up to date and reliable complete information. No warranties of any kind are expressed or implied. Readers acknowledge that the author is not engaging in the rendering of legal, financial, medical or professional advice.

By reading this document, the reader agrees that under no circumstances are we responsible for any loss- es, direct or indirect, which are incurred as a result of the use of information contained within this docu- ment, including, but not limited to, —errors, omissions, or inaccuracies.

Introduction

Having huge amount of debt can wreak havoc in your life. It can cause so much stress and it can lead to many problems. It can cause various emotional problems like depression, shame, anxiety, and anger.

Having too much debt can also lead to regret, anger, and frustration. It can ruin relationships and it can ruin your life. It can lead to eviction, bankruptcy, foreclosure, and even suicidal tendencies.

If you have too much debt, it is time to get out of it and reclaim the power that you have over your life. This book contains steps and strategies that will help you get out of debt. This book will help you identify the warning signs that are in debt trouble. Also, this book contains various steps and strategies that will help you get out of debt.

Getting out of debt is something that can seem like a daunting task. It is never an easy task and without the discipline it is almost impossible. The only way for people to get out of debt, is they have to first change the habits that had put them there in the first place. Debt isn't something that somebody forced upon you, whether it is college debt or credit card debt it doesn't matter.

1. Set Your Goals

Paying off debt is a goal in itself, so why do we have to think about goal setting any further?

Because goal-setting is a powerful psychological tool. Making steps to reach goals triggers our brains to release dopamine, the neurotransmitter that causes us to feel happy and satisfied. Having more goals that can be achieved at regular intervals produces a chemical chain reaction that helps you pay off debt faster.

And the goals you can set on the path to debt freedom are virtually endless. You'll have spending limits to target, earning goals, payment goals, lifestyle challenges to overcome, and even relationship goals. When you break down these processes and make goals around them, you'll find you reach the big goal faster.

To get my spending under control, I would try to "fast" from spending on certain things for weeks at a time. Every day I got closer to meeting my goal, I had more motivation to keep going. There were times every day that I wanted to give up, but with every day those moments got shorter and shorter. And by the end, I was so proud of myself I couldn't wait to take on the next challenge.

While there's no shortage of goals you can set, only focus on one or two at a time. Multitasking makes you less efficient. In Gary Keller's book, The One Thing, he proposes that by focusing on one thing at a time we actually get more done at a faster rate than when we're trying to juggle multiple goals.

Look at your problem areas, timeline, debts, etc. and write down the goals you want to accomplish that will help you pay off your debt faster and choose one or two to start with.

You can do this on the Day 3 worksheet in the free workbook that accompanies this book. Find it at modernfrugality.com/debtfreeworkbook[1].

1. http://modernfrugality.com/debtfreeworkbook

The Psychology of Goals

After your brainstorm, work on refining those goals. Because there are ways you can think about and write your goals to help you achieve them. Here are some things to consider:

Setting goals causes a shift in your identity. When you set a goal, your brain starts to associate your identity with the desired outcome. Say you set a goal to stop going to the mall every weekend. Your brain thinks you shouldn't be at the mall and will produce constant tension between reality and the goal. That tension will internally motivate you to do something else on the weekend. And if you do go to the mall, it won't bring you as much enjoyment as it used to.

If your goal is to spend better, start acting and making decisions like someone who makes good spending decisions. Your brain will support the change.

Shorter is better. With every achievement on the path to meeting your goal, your body releases sweet, sweet dopamine into your brain. And you now know that the more hits of dopamine your brain gets, the easier it'll be to stay focused and motivated.

Well, missing a goal has an equal, opposite reaction. The dopamine gets cut off and you'll feel like giving up. So make every effort to avoid that cutoff by breaking your ultimate debt payoff goal into smaller ones.

No goal is too small. Start by making a payment that's more than the minimum balance due, or transferring your emergency fund to an account that's harder to spend. Whatever it is, make the first few goals ridiculously easy so you can get that dopamine train running.

Setting goals fosters resourcefulness. The deadlines, numbers, and parameters associated with goals foster the ability to find quick and clever ways to overcome difficulties. Resourcefulness will force you to redefine what's possible and show you how much more you're capable of doing than you once thought.

People can get very creative when trying to reach their goals, so don't let difficulties derail you. Use them to learn and think outside the box.

Goal-Setting Methods

> Goal-setting researchers Gary Latham and Edwin Locke evaluated dozens of their own studies along with those of other scientists to see what kind of goals people followed through on the most. They found that the best goals are those that are specific and difficult, but not outrageously tough.

In order to ensure your goals are as effective as possible, there are several methods you can use to formulate them.

The SMART criteria is the most well-known. It helps you focus on the achievability of your goal.

· Specific: The goal should be clear and simple. You should be able to write it down concisely.

· Measurable: You should be able to easily track your progress.

· Achievable: The goal should be realistically achievable in your time frame.

· Relevant: For the purposes of this book, the goal should play a significant part in getting you closer to paying off your debt.

· Time-bound: The goal should have a deadline to give it a sense of urgency and importance.

People love the SMART criteria because it provides hyper-focused parameters that give tangible feedback on how you're progressing with your goals. But strict criteria don't work for everyone. If you want an acronym that's simpler but just as effective, try ABC.

- Achievable/Aim-High: The goal should be challenging, but achievable.

- Believable: Believe in yourself and your capacity to move closer to paying off debt.

- Committed: Commit to work on the goal on a daily basis.

The ABC method focuses more on the challenging aspect of the goal, which can help be a catalyst for meeting bigger goals faster. You should still be able to clearly write down your goal, but there's more flexibility. The drawback is that you have to have the resiliency to be OK if—and when—you occasionally fall short.

For either method, here are some tips for achieving your goals:

Write them down. George Wu, a professor of behavioral science, encouraged marathon runners to write down their finishing goal for an upcoming race. Most of them already had a goal in mind, but Wu found that the ones who actually wrote down their goals ended up running faster than the control group who did not. Just like the runners, you'll go faster by making your goals tangible.

Find "fresh start" moments. The first day of the year, month, or week are naturally "fresh start" moments that can make your goals more measurable. You can also choose special dates like a birthday or anniversary. The mistake you don't want to make in choosing your "fresh start" is to use it as an excuse to put off starting a goal. Make them meaningful but make them soon.

Share your goals. Don't just write down your goals for you to see. Share them with others, too. A great place to do this is on Instagram. Use hashtags like #debtfreejourney and #debtfreecommunity on your posts to connect with a large community of people paying off debt and be a part of their progress too.

1. How to Create a Livable Budget

There's no point in creating a budget you can't live with. That's why your budget has to reflect your needs, your finances, and your plans. There are dozens of different ways to budget and thousands of financial gurus bombarding you with advice. Go with whatever feels right for you and ignore everything else.

Your first budget won't be perfect. It may not even work. If that happens, don't give up on making a plan for your money; just scrap that budget and make a different one. It may take a little time to get this right, and when you do, you'll get a rush that comes from being in control of your money instead of worrying how you'll get through the month.

The Basic Budget Equation

Income and Expenses

No matter what type you choose, all budgets start in the same place with a very simple equation. Two main numbers will figure into your budget: income (the money coming in) and expenses (the money going out).

In its most basic sense the budget equation starts with income and subtracts expenses. If the result is positive, you have a surplus. If the result is negative, you have a shortfall. If the result is zero, you've successfully accounted for every dollar. No matter which result you get, creating a better plan for your money will bring you closer to your goals more quickly.

As straightforward as that two-part equation is, there are a lot of different ways to solve it. Pick whichever method feels the most comfortable for you. If you decide you don't like it for any reason (too much math, not enough detail, etc.), try a different method or create your own formula. Whichever approach you can stick with is the format that will work for you.

The Track Everything Budget

When you hear "budget," this traditional method is probably what comes to mind: tracking every expense individually to see how each measures up to your preset spending targets. This approach works well for detail-oriented people and people who really want to get a handle on their spending. It's also a good choice for budget newbies, because tracking everything is the only way to see where money is really going.

Luckily, software and apps can do all of the time-consuming tracking tasks so you won't have to devote too much time to your budget after you have everything set up. Once you've gotten a good handle on your finances, you can switch over to a more big-picture method if tracking everything becomes burdensome or unnecessary.

Where Did It Go?

Spending habits vary widely by generation, according to a 2016 report by the US Department of Labor. Millennials spent the most on motorcycles and musical instruments, but the least on ice cream. Gen Xers spent the most on almost everything, from alcohol to cleaning supplies to shoes. Baby boomers spent the most on pets, jewelry, and healthcare, but the least on furniture.

The 50–30–20 Budget

If you're comfortable with big spending buckets, the 50–30–20 budget plan might work well for you. Instead of drilling down to line-item expenses, this method takes a big-picture approach where all cash outflow gets sorted into three categories:

1. 50 percent to needs
2. 30 percent to wants
3. 20 percent to savings

The trick to using this budget is carefully separating out needs and wants. For example, apples and Pop-Tarts are both groceries, but Pop-Tarts wouldn't count as a "need."

What about debt? Minimum debt payments fall under the needs category, while extra debt payments get lumped in with savings.

The 80–20 Budget

Sometimes called the "pay yourself first" plan, the 80–20 budget separates savings from everything else. Every time you get paid, the first 20 percent goes straight into savings and the rest goes into one big spending pile. That doesn't mean all 20 percent has to go into a single savings vehicle; split it among your retirement savings, emergency fund, goal-based savings accounts, and extra debt payments. As with the other big-picture budgets, you can adjust the percentages to better suit your savings style.

The Zero-Sum Budget

With the zero-sum budget, money in equals money out every month. That doesn't mean you'll have no money in the bank at the end of the month, but it means you won't have any money left in your budget. That's because in this method, every dollar gets assigned to something: needs, wants, savings, or debt payment, for example.

To get started with this, you follow the traditional budget idea of writing down your monthly income and expenses (which include savings). The goal is for income and expenses to be equal—but it usually doesn't work out exactly that way the first time around. So if you bring in $4,000 a month, $4,000 will go out. If you happen to have any money left over at the end, you give it a job so you can get back to zero.

The "Debt Diet" Budget

Oprah's "Debt Diet," created with advice from financial experts, uses a five-category approach to budgeting. It's more detailed than just the simple 50–30–20 but not as cumbersome as tracking everything. Spending in each category is based on a percentage of your take-home pay. Remember, these percentages and categories are guidelines, and you can adjust them if they don't quite fit your life.

The five categories include:

1. Housing: 35 percent. This includes everything to do with your home, from the rent or mortgage payment to utilities, insurance, and repairs.

2. Transportation: 15 percent. Any expense related to your main means of transportation goes here, including things like car payments, gas, parking, oil changes, and public transportation costs.

3. Other living expenses: 25 percent. This catchall category covers everything else you spend money on, including things like food, clothing, vacations, concert tickets, electronics, and pet care.

4. Savings: 10 percent. If this seems low for covering retirement, emergency funds, and goals saving, remember that it comes from take-home pay, so any employer-based retirement contributions have already been made.

5. Debt paydown: 15 percent. This category covers student loan, credit card debt, personal loan, and extra principal payments toward your mortgage and car loan (the regular monthly payments were accounted for in the first two categories).

If you have another big, regular expense (such as child care or ongoing medical costs), add in a sixth category. Pull the funding for that from housing, transportation, and other expenses rather than from savings or debt paydown.

Two Ways To Balance

Increase Income or Cut Expenses

When it comes to balancing your budget, you have two choices: cut expenses or increase income. Most old-fashioned budgeting books and financial experts go straight for expense cutting, advising you to do things like make your own coffee and get rid of Netflix, but that's a much more difficult way to go. It's often easier to increase income than cut expenses, creating more room in your budget for the things you want to spend your money on.

The best budgets do a little of each: increase income and cut out unintentional or unnecessary spending (things you don't even realize you're spending money—or too much money—on). When you take that double-sided approach, you'll be less likely to feel deprived and more likely to make quick financial progress that moves you closer to your goals.

Bump Up Income For More Financial Freedom

Bringing in more money is a great way to free up space in your budget, especially if you've been living paycheck to paycheck. You'll probably have more control over this side of the equation, which makes it less frustrating to focus on than digging around for more places to cut back. Plus, that extra income cushion can help you avoid late and missed payments, which can save you money in fees and penalties, automatically lowering your expenses.

Whether you find a way to increase your income at your current job, find a lucrative side gig, start using apps that pay cash, or some combination of income-boosting strategies, you'll make more headway toward your goals. If you're looking for a permanent boost, start developing income streams, investments of time or money that you set up today to provide income later. The more of these income streams you create, the less work you'll have to do to keep the income flowing.

What You Could Do with an Extra $100

As little as $100 goes further than you think. If you earn an extra $100 a month, you could build a $1,000 emergency fund in less than a year, make extra student loan payments and save thousands of dollars in interest, or invest it and let it bring in even more money for you.

Trim Expenses Where You Can

The number one rule of budgeting (of financial health, really) is spending less than your income. Even if you're already doing that, you may still be overspending, and that can keep you from reaching your financial goals and building wealth. Review your spending for a few months and look for expenses that are higher than you expected or that you didn't even realize you were paying. If you notice overspending—meaning spending more money than you intended or could afford—in any budget category, that's your starting point for cutbacks.

That doesn't mean you need to pinch every penny, buy only no-brand groceries, and stop having fun. Rather, it calls for putting a stop to any spending that doesn't serve your goals and cutting any expenses that don't add value to your life. Every dollar you don't spend on something you don't really need (or even want) can now be used toward what you would rather have, whether that's a house in five years or more money for going out with your friends this weekend.

Live With The Surplus, Not On It

Virtually everyone spends up to his or her income, and when that income increases he or she bumps up spending, a phenomenon called lifestyle creep. There's nothing wrong with that as long as you're aware of it, all of your financial goals are being met, you're not taking on more debt, and you're not constantly worried about money. If you're making a decision to boost your lifestyle, rather than just falling into it, you'll retool your budget to make sure spending doesn't spiral out of control.

But just imagine what your finances would look like if you didn't do that—or at least didn't let your spending creep all the way up.

Consider this: You get a hefty raise, and instead of buying a better car or moving into a nicer apartment, you don't. Instead, you use that surplus to supercharge your debt paydown or stash it in savings and investments. Now instead of spending more just because you can, you're making the conscious choice to build personal wealth.

Saving Is Your Number One Expense

The Path to Wealth

Financial comfort starts with savings. Once you have some money put aside, and you aren't desperately waiting for your next paycheck to pay bills, a whole new financial world will open up to you. You'll have more freedom and more choices, and those will only grow along with your savings.

This is the true path to wealth: holding on to your money instead of spending it. That's why your highest-priority expense is stashing money in some form of savings account. It doesn't matter if you save $10 or $200 at a time; what matters is getting into the habit of keeping some of your money for yourself. Once you start a savings habit, you'll be amazed at how fast your money accumulates, and that may inspire you to put even more money away.

Tap Into The Power Of Compounding

When it comes to building a sizeable nest egg, you need as much time on your side as possible. The more time you have, the bigger your savings will grow—even if you stop adding to the account—thanks to a powerful wealth-growing trick known as compounding.

Here's how compounding works. You put $100 into a savings account, and it earns $2 in interest (that's a 2 percent interest rate). Now you have $102, which earns $2.04 in interest, bumping your new account balance up to $104.04, even though you haven't added any more money to your savings. (You'll find the highest interest rates for savings accounts through credit unions or online banks.)

With the magic of compounding, you can let your money do all the work for you. Over time, your money starts to grow faster and faster because you're earning interest on a higher balance all the time.

That's the secret key to building wealth: time. When it comes to your savings goals, more time means more money. There is no second chance to capture the power of compounding. Time makes all the difference, so use all of the time you have and start saving right now.

Savings Priority 1: Get Your Free Money

If you have a 401(k) plan through work and your employer offers a match, take it. That means contributing enough of your own money to get the maximum match amount. If you don't, you are leaving free money on the table.

An employer match is extra money that your employer contributes to your retirement account based on the amount you contribute. For example, your employer could offer to match up to 3 percent of your salary in 401(k) contributions. If you earn $50,000, your employer would contribute a maximum of $1,500 (3 percent of $50,000). To get the full $1,500 match, you would have to contribute $1,500 of your money into the account. If you only contributed $500, the match would be $500, and you'd be losing out on $1,000 of free money.

Savings Priority 2: Take Advantage Of Compounding

Your retirement account contributions don't need to stop at the match. You can contribute up to the legal maximum, supercharging your future nest egg. Not only will your contributions lower your current tax bill—unless you contribute to a Roth IRA or Roth 401(k) account—but the earnings will grow tax-deferred. That means you won't pay a penny in taxes until you start taking the money out, which helps your money grow faster through compounding.

The more money you stash in retirement accounts early on, the bigger your nest egg will grow—even if you contribute less overall than someone who started ten years later. You can't go back in time to take advantage of compounding, so put away as much as you can as soon as you can to let your money grow as much as it can.

Savings Priority 3: Emergency Fund

Your car breaks down. Your dog chews up your smartphone. You lose your job. Unexpected expenses or income shortfalls crop up, and paying for them can put a serious crimp in your budget unless you're prepared with some emergency funds to cover them. People with even modest emergency savings take on less debt and have more financial flexibility than people with no emergency fund, giving them an edge when it comes to building wealth.

How big a safety net do you need in your emergency fund? Three months of living expenses (necessities) will give you enough breathing room to handle most emergencies while you work to get your finances back on track. To make sure you don't dip into this fund for regular expenses, keep it in an interest-bearing savings account that is not linked to your regular checking account. In fact, keeping it in a different bank adds an extra step to using that money, helping ensure you won't touch it unless you really need to.

That's Not an Emergency

Periodic or large expected expenses (such as a property tax bill or scheduled car maintenance) are not emergencies, so don't pull from your emergency fund to cover them. You know these costs are coming and at least approximately when, so you can plan to put money aside to cover them. Leave your emergency fund for things that are truly unexpected.

Savings Priority 4: Savings Goals

When you set your SMART goals, some of them were probably linked to savings. Each goal you set came with a dollar amount and a time frame, making it easy to figure out how much you'd need to contribute every month to stay on track. For example, if a two-week tour of Scottish castles costs $3,500 and you want to get there in two years, you'd need to save $146 a month.

After you've figured that out for all of your goals, add them up to figure out how much you'd need to save each month in total. Chances are, you won't be able to meet all of your goals by their deadlines (especially because they come after retirement and emergency savings on the priority scale). Even if you intend to start saving for only your top-ranked goals, they still may call for more funding than you have available. That calls for a little goal editing, which usually involves extended timelines. Maybe you won't be able to replace your car in five years without taking on debt and get to Scotland in two years, but moving the trip out another year or two makes both goals possible.

Now that you know how much you'll devote to each goal, you need a place to house that savings. To meet multiple goals, it's helpful to have a different space for each—but dealing with several savings accounts can be a big savings turn-off. Many online banks offer the option of "sub-savings," which lets you allocate your money among different goals all inside a single bank account. SmartyPig (an online savings bank, www.smartypig.com), for example, lets you set up different savings goals, complete with target balances and end dates. Every transfer into the primary savings account gets split up according to the goals you've set, and they automatically stop when any goal has been reached.

Keep Yourself From Dipping In

One of the biggest barriers to savings is withdrawals. If you tend to dip into your savings for any reason other than their purpose (for example, tapping into emergency savings to pay for a party you hosted with your credit card), you'll need to find ways to stop that negative financial habit. When sheer willpower isn't doing the trick, try these tricks to safeguard your savings:

• Name your savings. Put a label on every savings account you have (emergency, house down payment, fun money, whatever it's for). That makes you less likely to withdraw the money for any other reason.

• Lock it up. Put the money for longer-term savings goals into time-locked CDs. You'll earn a little more interest and have less (but not no) access to that cash until the CD comes due.

• Hide it from yourself. Set up automatic deposits into the account, and include those in a different budget category. Don't connect the account to any apps or other bank accounts, and you just might forget you have it.

• Nix the debit card. If you don't have easy access to the cash, you won't be as quick to withdraw it. Set it up so you actually have to go into the bank to take out money.

Use whatever strategies you can to keep yourself from raiding savings, and you'll see your money stack up much more quickly.

Set Your Spending Priorities

You Do You

Setting spending priorities is about figuring out what's most important to you.

Maybe you'd rather take a three-week beach vacation than buy a new car, or maybe the convenience of takeout every night tops a road trip to Coachella. Ranking your spending priorities helps make sure the things you really care about are covered in your budget and not crowded out by more mindless purchases. Spending priorities don't cover only big-ticket items; they factor into daily spending as well.

The key here is to spend your money on purpose. Pay attention to what you're buying, and take a second to consider the life cost (what else you could do with that money) as well as the financial cost. Then decide which is more important to you—and you've just set a spending priority.

Separate Needs And Wants

It may feel like you need that latte every morning, but in the world of budgets, it counts as a want. Figuring out the difference between what you want and what you need is an important part of constructing a budget you can really live with. It's easy to confuse wants and needs, but when you break it down, needs include only the absolute essentials: food, clothing, shelter, medical care, child care, transportation for work (or school), and minimum payments on your debt. Everything else is a want.

To be clear, you need food to live; you don't need Thai takeout three times a week. You need clothes, but you don't need cashmere sweaters or twenty pairs of shoes. That Thai takeout and those cashmere sweaters are wants disguised as needs, and they can sneak through as high-priority budget items if you aren't careful. Make sure to label those types of purchases as wants so they don't bust your budget.

Don't worry: there's most definitely a place in your budget for wants. They just have a lower priority than the things that you really need to live.

The Pyramid Of Needs

When your budget is supertight and you're struggling to make ends meet, it's critical to prioritize your needs (wants are totally off the table here). If you can't meet all of your financial needs, some of your bills won't get paid, so you need to make sure the bills you do not skip are for things you could not get by without. Your priorities may be different here and there, but in most cases, this is the order to use for covering your bills:

1. Housing. Your number one priority is paying the rent or mortgage to keep a roof over your head.

2. Utilities. Having water, power, phone, and (for many people) Internet is priority number two.

3. Other home-related expenses. Any obligations related to your home, like property taxes and insurance, come next, especially if not paying them could result in losing your home.

4. Things you need to get to work. Anything connected to keeping your job or running your business—car payments, child care, gas—comes next in the list.

5. Minimum loan payments. Avoid expensive late fees, penalty interest rates, and other costs associated with default.

Any money that's left after these critical expenses are covered can go toward paying your other bills. (You may have noticed that food was not on this list; that's because the focus was on paying bills.)

Understand Opportunity Costs

Every time you buy something you don't need, you're sacrificing the chance to do something else with that money. Whatever you're giving up is the opportunity cost (or life cost) of that purchase. So while it may feel like you're sacrificing when you force yourself to pass up a splurge, it's really the opposite: when you splurge, you're sacrificing your goals.

For example, stopping at the local donut shop every morning on the way to work costs about $15 a week, or nearly $800 a year (if you pay cash, about $100 more if you pay with credit and don't pay your bill in full every month). Think about all the things you could do with $800—those are the opportunity costs.

When you feel the urge to buy anything that you don't need, whether it's a $3 cupcake or a $200 pair of shoes, think about the opportunities you're giving up. It'll take longer and cost more to pay down credit card debt. Your trip to Thailand will get pushed back another month (or six). If you still decide to spend the money now, that's okay because you've considered the opportunity cost and made a conscious choice about your purchase.

Go For The Guaranteed Win

Every month, your money gets pulled in dozens of different directions that all feel important and that can leave your goals short. When that happens, it can be hard to figure out how to split up your goals money. Do you put less money in each? Do you put some on the back burner? The best way to figure out your solution is to prioritize your goals so you're prepared to handle occasional budget shortfalls.

One of the best strategies here is to go for guaranteed wins, putting money toward goals that reward you in concrete terms. For example, paying down debt is a guaranteed win because you absolutely save interest going forward. Beefing your retirement savings falls into this category, too, especially if your employer offers matching contributions—an instant guaranteed win. By choosing these guaranteed goal victories, you'll actually be able to meet your other goals more quickly.

Spend Less Than You Make

Bring Back Some Change

It's the number one most important thing you can do to take control of your money and build lasting wealth, but it's also one of the hardest things for most people to do: spend less money than you make. There's constant pressure, both external and internal, to buy more, and it can be very hard to resist. In fact, the only way to thwart that pressure is to be aware of it and turn away.

Spending more money than you make does more than blow your budget. It puts your financial future at risk, forcing you to keep paying for the past instead of saving for the future. Overspending means that you are in debt, usually high-interest credit card debt, which shrinks your budget and traps you in a debt cycle. By putting an immediate stop to overspending, and committing to spending less than you earn, you're taking the most critical step toward getting your finances under control.

Credit Cards Enable Overspending

You can't overspend money—actual money—because once you part with it, it's gone. Credit cards let you overspend without a thought.

Consider this scene: You bring $60 (your budgeted amount) to the grocery store. When the cashier rings you up, the total comes to $68. You have only $60 on you, so you have to put something back. But if the same situation happened when you were carrying a credit card, you'd just buy the extra stuff, whether it ran $8 or $38 over your grocery budget.

Debit Cards Do It Too

Debit cards also make it easier to overspend, but with a set stopping point. Once you've drained your bank account, you can't spend any more. But until that point, using your debit card can push you over budget and even lead to expensive overdraft fees.

Until you can stick to your budget even when you're carrying credit cards—meaning you'd still put things back until your total came down to $60 in our example—don't take credit cards with you when you go shopping.

Try A Spending Freeze

One way to knock down spending is with a temporary spending freeze. Here's how it works: for a preplanned period of time, usually no more than a month or two, you spend money only on absolute necessities. A move like this will bring your budget into sharp focus, which can help you weed out excess spending and jump-start progress toward your goals.

It can be hard to stick to a spending freeze, especially in the beginning, but it does get easier over time. In fact, many people who try a temporary freeze get so used to living without wants that they end up reducing their spending permanently.

What expenses would be allowable during a freeze? Just the bare necessities, including:

- Housing (rent or mortgage payments, gas, electric, and water, for example)
- Groceries (avoid prepared foods and snack foods)
- Transportation (to and from work or school, avoid unnecessary travel)
- Medical costs (such as prescriptions and doctor visits)

For your best chance of success, avoid shopping in real life and online. When you grocery shop, work from and stick to a list, and limit trips to the store to one per week.

A Family Freeze Challenge

If you have a couple's or family budget, you all have to agree to the spending freeze, or it won't work as well. To get other family members more excited (or at least less resistant) about these temporary extreme cutbacks, you can turn it into a contest, with a splurge prize for the winner once the freeze is lifted.

Your temporary sacrifices offer the perfect opportunity for an extreme budget reset. The freeze will clarify what you really need and what you can do without on your journey to more solid financial footing.

Set Up Conscious Spending Rules

If it's hard for you to pass up great deals and impulse buys, set up conscious spending rules to rein in those habits. These rules force you to think more about the money you're spending so you have to make a deliberate choice to make a purchase. Here are three examples of impulse-thwarting spending rules.

1. The "wait for it" rule. If you want to buy something that costs more than $100 (or $200 or $50, depending on your situation), wait a week before you do it. Use that wait time to figure out if you still want the something. If you do, look for a way that you can get it for less money.

2. The "indecision decision" rule. If you can't decide between two things you want to buy, don't get either. When you really want something, the choice will be clear.

3. The "something in, something out" rule. Any time you buy an item you don't need, something you already have (something comparable) has to be given away, donated, or sold. If you're trying to downsize, make it a "two-out for one-in" rule.

Putting these types of rules in place will slow things down and get you used to thinking twice before you buy anything you don't need.

1. The Basics of Credit Card Debt and Bankruptcy

People know the basics of credit cards. Once you are approved, you then receive your card and activate it. You can use it for pretty much anything, such as purchasing groceries, clothing, or paying bills. The nice part is that you only have to make the minimum payment every month to keep yourself out of credit card debt. Unfortunately, it is this kind of thinking that often leads people into credit card debt.

Below are some basic points that most people don't realize about credit card debt.

1. Know When Short-Term Loans Make More Sense

Sometimes we need to get some cash or find a way to pay a few bills quickly. Many people turn to credit cards for these reasons. They receive their answer within minutes, and their card will arrive in the mail in about five to seven business days. However, sometimes it is better to go to your bank and talk to a loan advisor instead. If you need a couple of thousand dollars to pay off your medical bills, so they aren't sent to a collection agency, it might be best to take out a short-term loan from your local bank or credit union.

2. Credit Card Debt Can Result in Bad Credit

Paying off your credit cards in a less than timely manner or missing the minimum payment aren't the only things that are going to result in you having bad credit; having credit cards that hold high balances can also increase your chances of bad credit. In fact, you should make sure you always have at least 30 percent of your credit limit available.

While it is almost impossible in today's world, your best chance of keeping yourself from having bad credit is by remaining as free of debt as you possibly can.

3. Owing Is the Easy Part, and the Hard Part Is Paying Credit Cards Back

The reality of life is that you never really know what is going to happen. You could have a job for a couple of decades and then find out that you are randomly laid off due to cutbacks. You could have an illness spike that causes surgery. There are a lot of situations that can cause you to think you can start paying your credit cards every other month so you can make other bills. You could also find yourself struggling to pay the full minimum balance, so you may decide to pay about half of it every month.

Another reason your debt will climb is due to your credit limit increasing. This makes you feel mentally secure about being able to purchase your new couch on your credit card because your limit just increased by $500. However, what you are really doing is creating more credit card debt and causing your minimum monthly payment to increase. On top of this, your interest is going to compound, which makes it increase.

4. You Will Find Yourself Spending More Than You Make

It doesn't matter how responsible you are with credit cards; one of the biggest reasons people find themselves in credit card debt is because they spend more than they make every month. Credit cards are very tempting because they provide you with the thought that you can just pay it back later or make smaller payments on the purchase every month. Although, in reality, you should never spend more than what your monthly income is.

5. Most People Use Credit Cards to Handle Emergencies

It is common for people to tell others that a credit card is only used for emergencies, but do you really keep in mind what a true emergency is? Most people live paycheck to paycheck. Therefore, when they see their checking account balance drop low, and there are several days before their next payday, they will start to think about each purchase they make and wonder if they should use their credit card as it is considered an emergency or a need

6. People Think as Long as They Make The Minimum Payment, They Will Be Fine

In reality, you always want to make sure you pay more than the minimum payment. Think of it this way: if you have a $75 minimum payment, at least 25 percent of what you pay is going to go toward interest and fees. This means that you are really only putting 75 percent of your payment toward paying off your debt. Depending on how much you owe, this could be a low amount. If you aren't careful, you could find yourself going over your credit limit, which means your credit card company will charge you their over-the-limit fee.

Furthermore, only paying the minimum payment is going to take you years to pay off. It really doesn't matter how low you feel your credit limit is versus how high you believe your minimum monthly payment is. It can still take at least a couple of years to pay off your debt, providing you stop using your credit card.

Bankruptcy

Only an organization or individual that is unable to completely honor its financial obligation or make payment to its creditor files for bankruptcy. This goes to say that a bankruptcy filing is a legal course of action taken by a company or person to relieve themselves from debt obligations where all outstanding debt of the company is evaluated and paid from the company's assets. As legal proceeding goes, bankruptcy is carried out to give individuals and businesses freedom from debt they have already incurred and at the same time provide creditors with the opportunity to get their debts paid. It can be said to allow for a fresh start by forgiving debts that cannot be paid and at the same time offering creditors a substantive opportunity to get methods of repayment based on the available assets of a person or business that can be liquidated.

Theoretically, this can mean that the ability to file for bankruptcy can benefit the whole economy by giving businesses and individuals a second chance to have the utmost access to consumer credit and by providing creditors with a reliable measure of debt repayment. Once there is the successful completion of a bankruptcy proceeding, the debtor is to be relieved of their obligation from the debt that has been incurred before filing for bankruptcy. However, it will be on their credit record that such a person had acquired debts before and filed for bankruptcy. This information is going to remain on the record for about seven to ten years, depending on the type of bankruptcy filed.

Types of Bankruptcy

There are two types of bankruptcy.

1. **Debt Discharge.** This is simply the cancellation of debt, thanks to bankruptcy. Based on the Internal Revenue Code, a debtor must add into their gross income the discharge of indebtedness, after which a court must have discharged his/her debt upon meeting all conditions. However, if a debtor should refuse financial counseling, commits a crime, fails to fully explain the loss of his/her assets, provides false information during court proceedings, or basically disobeys the orders of the court, a judge can rightfully refuse to discharge the debt of such a person.
2. **The Payment Plan.** This is a kind of bankruptcy filed, where a debtor and his/her lawyer submit to the court a kind of repayment plan of how the debtor plans to pay off his/her debts in three to five years. This plan is dependent on the

debtor's income, food, and utilities, tax, and healthcare expenses. Should the court approve the plan, the debtor proceeds to make the payments required as stipulated in the plan. If such a debtor is consistent with the payments, the remaining debts will be discharged at the end of the three to five-year period. The payments are made to a trustee from the bankruptcy court that then proceeds to pay the creditors while getting a commission too.

Concerning business, the two types of bankruptcy are:

1. **Reorganization Bankruptcy.** This is a kind of bankruptcy filed meant to help business owners who have serious issues with their business but still have regular income and valuable assets and reorganize the business. The business is allowed to continue its operations with the court's supervision of course. The creditors aren't allowed to interfere with the debtors during the supervision. Business owners will have to share their reorganization plan with the creditors providing them part of the payment. But if the creditors do not agree with the plan, they have the right to file a competing plan.
2. **Farming Bankruptcy.** It is a type of bankruptcy specially designed for farmers of the same family. It is to help the family reorganize their farming business as well as settle all their debts. The unpredictable nature of farming and seasonal moods is factors that are seriously considered.

Implications of Bankruptcy

Before you consider filing for bankruptcy, you need to first understand how it works, as well as the pros and cons. It's not a simple issue that can be done quickly but has a complex side only a bankruptcy attorney understands. It would be best if you find out everything you can before filing for bankruptcy. Find below the consequences of filing bankruptcy.

Pros

1. **Discharge.** Getting debts discharged is one major reason people file for bankruptcy. And when such debt is discharged, erasing all your debts as well as preventing creditors from collecting further payments from you, the debtor becomes relieved. It's one huge advantage of filing for bankruptcy. Not everyone who filed for debt discharge is granted. If you owe debts on alimony, tax liabilities, or child support, filing for bankruptcy would be a waste of time. Such debts are not forgiven nor discharged.
2. **Automatic Stay.** Here is another advantage to being enjoyed when a bankruptcy is filed. It is a situation whereby the person who files for bankruptcy becomes automatically protected from the creditors and the property over the collection of debts. The protection stays until the court finally decrees the debts to be honored and forgiven or discharged. In a situation that involves divorce proceedings, the automatic stay might be lifted.

Cons

1. **Loss of Property.** There's a possibility that a bankruptcy filer might lose his/her property if the court decides it's valuable enough to pay off the debt owed. This could happen if you include your property in your case to the bankruptcy trustee. Your creditor could have higher leverage in trying to get your property, especially if you used such property initially as collateral.
2. **Credit Score.** Another downside to filing for bankruptcy is that it decreases your credit score. Loaners will only see you

as risky when they check your credit history because filing for bankruptcy won't in any way clean up your debt history even though your debt is canceled. However, it's a better option than acquiring debt. You can always rebuild your credit score later.

3. **Privacy.** If you're sensitive about your privacy, filing for bankruptcy might not be for you, and this explains why you must do your research if you want to file for bankruptcy. You can either prepare yourself against the consequences or look for other options. When you file a bankruptcy case, every detail about your financial statements becomes public. In other words, anyone can access your personal information without your permission. The amount you owed, who your creditors were, and your bankruptcy schedule can be assessed easily by anyone. It can be such a big deal if you cherish your privacy.

1. Is your mortgage a good or bad debt?

It can be either, depending on your circumstances. Here's a quick reminder of the three criteria that all good debts must meet:

1. It makes you more money than what it's costing you to have it, **and...**
2. It has high odds of turning a profit, **and...**
3. It's money that you can afford to lose.

Now we'll take a look at a couple of examples to illustrate the difference between a mortgage that's good debt and a mortgage that's bad debt.

Example 1

Sara has saved up $60,000 cash and is debating whether or not she ought to avoid taking on a mortgage and just continue to rent a house, or if she ought to buy one.

She plans on living in the same home for at least 20 years — all of her family is in this town, there are lots of jobs, and she loves the area. In other words, if she buys, she'll be holding onto the property for the long term, which makes it very likely that her home would be worth more than what she paid for it by the time she's ready to consider selling.

She's currently paying $1850 per month to rent a house. Utilities are not included.

She could buy a comparable home for $300,000. If she puts a $60,000 down payment towards it, and gets a 30-year mortgage at 4% interest, her monthly mortgage payments will be about $1140 per month. Additional expenses that she'll have to take on that she didn't have to worry about when renting include the following:

- Property taxes
- Maintenance and repairs

For the purposes of our example, Sara's property taxes are expected to be $3000 per year, which averages out to $250/month. And she's budgeting 1.5% of her home's value for maintenance and repairs each year, which averages out to $375 per month (i.e. [300,000 x 0.015]/12) So now we're looking at a total of about $1765 per month in housing expenses if she buys a house (i.e. $1140 mortgage payment + $250 property taxes + $375 maintenance and repairs = $1765).

Given this situation, the odds are good that she's better off buying compared to renting. Aside from the obvious break-even on monthly expenses, the really big advantage of buying is that 20 years from now, she'll have paid off about $187,000 worth of the purchase price (with $113,000 left to pay off).

Assuming that housing prices go up at approximately the rate of inflation (see Appendix, 4% is a decent estimate for average annual inflation), her home will be worth about $657,336 at that time. So if she sells, she'll pocket about $544,000 before taking into account any realtor commissions or other expenses incurred when selling her home.

Whereas if she rented, she'd get nothing.

In this case, her mortgage can be considered to be good debt. In fact, it's a very good debt. The risk is so low and the profit is so large compared to the zero she'd get by renting that buying a home is a no brainer for her.

Criteria 1 is met because she's going to spend the same amount of money on housing whether she buys or rents, and she'll end up making money if she sells 20 years from now as planned.

Criteria 2 is met because given her numbers and the fact that she plans on holding onto the property for 20 years she has high odds of making a profit compared to renting (because it's highly unlikely that her property will be worth less than what she paid for it when she sells).

Criteria 3 is met because she can afford to lose the money. If a freak calamity (ex. natural disaster for which insurance won't cover her) happened that destroyed her home, she could afford to make the mortgage payments in addition to paying rent on a new place to live. Sure, she'd have to downsize dramatically to pull this off, but she could do it.

Example 2

Jim is currently renting. His job transfers him to a new city every 2-3 years. He hates paying rent and is tempted to buy. So he considers the pros and cons.

It turns out that while he can buy a place for the same monthly costs as he's paying in rent, his odds of making a profit aren't good enough to make him pull the trigger. This is because he's in a city with a volatile real estate market where prices have a history of making large swings over short periods of time. In 2013 prices went up by 15%, in 2014 they went up by 5%, and in 2015 they fell by 20%. Who knows what'll happen this year and next before he'd have to sell.

In this case, buying a condo or house doesn't meet our second criteria for good debt because the risk of losing money if he buys for such a short period of time is too high.

He opts to rent.

On the other hand, if Jim could have bought a well-maintained home and been sure that he'd hold onto it for at least 20 years, the risk of losing money on the purchase would have been next to nothing, because even in a volatile market, over a long period of time the general trend is for housing to go up at approximately the rate of inflation. (You can read more about this in the Appendix.)

Mortgages and you

If you have a mortgage now, or are thinking of getting one in the future, be sure to run the numbers for yourself and determine whether or not a mortgage meets the criteria for good debt in your situation.

We all have a different tolerance for risk. We all have varying incomes. Some people can handle a loss (both financially and emotionally) from buying a home more easily than others. Some people can mitigate any financial risks involved with buying a home (ex. over-budget repairs) by earning more money or cutting expenses. Others can't.

Always calculate the expected expenses and potential profit compared to renting for yourself, weigh the pros and cons of available choices, and make the best decision you can based on your individual financial situation and temperament.

Trailers and Mobile Homes

Although trailers and mobile homes can be used for housing, they're not in the same category as a house or condominium when it comes to being an investment. This is because unlike houses and condominiums, trailers and mobile homes tend to decrease in value with time, rather than increase. As far as profit potential goes, it's comparable to living in a car.

The exception is if you buy a cheap one for cash that's already lost pretty much all of its value. In other words, when you sell, you figure you'll get all of your money back. If doing so will cost you less than renting, this might be worth it if you want to live really frugally for a few years and save up some cash.

Obviously this doesn't mean that buying a trailer or mobile home is always a bad idea. Just as with anything else, everyone's circumstances are different and there are always nuances to consider.

If buying one of these will save you money and it meets the three criteria for good debt compared to renting, then by all means go for it if it's what you want to do. But if not, it's probably best avoided.

How to know if you can afford to buy a home

Assuming you've come to the conclusion that a mortgage is likely to be a good debt for you, here are some factors to consider when deciding how much to spend. Because if you over-stretch your finances by taking on mortgage payments that are too high, you'll struggle more than necessary to pay off your bad debts because too much money will be going towards housing.

First, throw out any notion of one-size-fits-all guidelines. Despite claims to the contrary, there aren't any.

For example, it's commonly said that as long as your debt to income ratio isn't greater than 43%, you're doing fine.

Sure, if you're making $150,000 a year, and are reasonably careful with your money, odds are that you can easily afford to spend $64,500 a year (about 43%) of it on a combination of mortgage payments, a car loan, and whatever else you borrowed money for, and still have enough leftover to pay for necessities like food, utility bills, healthcare, and clothing. But that's not the case for people making lower incomes.

Martha bought a condo in good times, and the mortgage payments are $645 a month. Even though she's a single mom of two kids, it was easy to afford this at the time because she had a decently paying job. But then she got laid off during a downturn in the economy, and the only job she could find now pays a paltry $18,000 per year.

In theory, since she has no other debts, she should be just fine, right?

Because her mortgage payments (her only debt) only add up to 43% of her income (i.e. $645/mo x 12 months/$18,000 x 100 = 43%)

But Martha's not doing fine at all. She only has $855 per month (pre-tax) leftover to cover basic necessities like food, clothing, utilities, and medical expenses — and she's finding it very difficult to pay for all that for her small family of three.

One-size-fits-all plans are flawed. They fail to account for the differences in disposable income between high and low income earners.

Other flawed rules

Another number that's tossed around a lot is the 30% rule. This rule originated from the 1969 Brook Amendment to the Housing and Urban Development Act of 1968, which introduced the idea that rent for public housing should be no more than 25% of the family income. In 1981, Congress increased this figure to 30%. *Sources say*[2] these increases were put into place in the hopes that they'd allow rental property owners to better afford maintenance for their properties.

It's dismaying that the reasoning for the 30% rule had nothing to do with how much the average homeowner could afford, yet it's commonly used as a guideline for determining exactly that. What craziness!

Even worse, is that this 30% standard is now commonly recommended to home buyers as a one-size-fits-all way of deciding how high of a mortgage payment they can afford.

Don't be fooled

So the next time you come across a one-size-fits-all rule for how much to spend on mortgage payments, look at it with skepticism. For most people, I recommend that you aim to spend LESS than these rules dictate. Spending less will allow you more flexibility with your finances and make it easier to afford a bit of fun in your life.

As for how much less you ought to spend, there's only one way to figure that out. You've got to go back to basics. Track your spending and income. Find out how much of your spending is optional and how much of it is for non-negotiable necessities, including savings. Only then will you know how much you can truly afford to spend on a mortgage (or even rent for that matter!).

How fast should you pay off your home

2. *https://www.census.gov/housing/census/publications/who-can-afford.pdf*

The less debt you have, the less financial risk you're exposed to. After you've paid off your bad debts, plow the money that's been freed up into getting rid of your mortgage as quickly as possible.

Imagine this: what if housing prices fall by 50% like they did in many areas back in 2008? And what if jobs dry up and many people, including you, have decided that the best option is to move somewhere else with a better job market? If your mortgage has been paid off, even if you had to move for a better job market on short notice and sell your home for less than you paid for it, you'll probably be okay (granted, not happy about it, but you certainly won't have to worry about going bankrupt over such a thing). Whereas for someone who hasn't paid off their home, being forced by circumstances to sell during a price crash could be stressful if the balance owing is more than the proceeds generated by selling it.

Action step

If you have a mortgage (or are thinking of getting one) run the numbers, assess the risk, and find out if it meets the three criteria for good debt in your unique situation. If it does, that's great. But if it doesn't, you need to take action.

What to do if your mortgage is bad debt

If you have a mortgage and come to the conclusion that it's bad debt, you need to get rid of it as soon as possible. Here are some options for doing that:

Consider selling it and cutting your losses now if the following three criteria are met:

· you don't think it's likely that you'll be able to hang onto the home long enough for it to turn a profit compared to renting, and,

· the losses are expected to continue to grow with time, and,

- you won't suffer any negative financial consequences such as bankruptcy if you do so

Consider keeping it and paying it off ASAP if the following two criteria are met:

- selling it would ruin your credit because it would force you to declare bankruptcy (for example, if you owe more on the mortgage than the house is worth and you can't afford to repay the difference to the lender), and,

- you can afford to continue making payments

Remember that if your current mortgage is bad debt, that doesn't mean that would be the case with any and all mortgages. For example, say your mortgage is bad debt because you accidentally bought a home that required mountains of expensive repairs that killed any hope of ever making a profit over time. If you bought a well-maintained home that only required normal levels of repairs, that could be enough to turn a mortgage into good debt for you. Or, say your mortgage is bad debt because you bought a home that's too expensive. If you sell it and replace it with a less expensive home, the numbers may work out in your favor this time and turn a profit over the long term compared to renting.

Don't assume all mortgages are good debt, or that all mortgages are bad debt for you. Run the numbers and assess the risk each and every time — every mortgage situation is different, even for the same person.

What to do if your mortgage is good debt

There's no one-size-fits-all rule for how much you should spend on a home or how high of a mortgage payment you can afford to make. Rules such as the 43% limit for a debt to income ratio or a 30%-of-gross-income upper limit for mortgage or rent payments should not be accepted as automatically affordable for you personally.

Unfortunately, there are no short cuts here. The only way to know for sure what your personal limit should be is to run the numbers. Track your earnings. Track your spending. Make an informed decision about what you can afford after you've gathered all the facts.

Figure out if your mortgage is good or bad debt in your situation, and take action based on that. Everyone is different.

1. Secret to Eliminate Debt Fast

Discovering yourself somewhat (or possibly a lot) indebted today? Is it affecting your feeling as well as your personal lifestyle? Join the club, if you feel just like you're falling in quicksand, but certainly do not worry. I am planning to review how to get out of debt as rapidly and effortlessly that you can, and help you save some money in the act, so continue reading.

Setting yourself up for debt is not difficult to do. In these financial situations, many families find it robust to carry the duty of dropping their jobs and having less spending cash, and getting a little bit into debt appears ordinary during the time. It could become a significant supplier of strain once you get so serious and don't know ways to get out of debt.

Fortunately, there are lots of points you can do to begin along the right path towards a debt- life. Here are 4 considerations to consider:

1. Create a plan: a real plan is never created by 2/3 of people who want to get out of debt. It may come as not surprising that having a great strategy is vital if you'd like to attain of being debt free your target.

2. Cut your credit cards up. It might be a good idea to leave one for emergencies, but lowering them up is an image of your commitment to living within your means. Begin play the role of more realistic by what you are able and spending cash.

3. Request a lowered interest rate from your creditors. You would certainly be surprised at just how many of them will be ready to assist you out if you call them and inform them about your approach (step 1). Another option gets a debt consolidation mortgage or moving your debt to the credit card that's the bottom rate.

4. Begin going up, beginning with the very best rates of interest first, and paying down the debts one at any given time.

Learning to get out of debt is not difficult should you remain focused on a proven strategy. The most critical stage is creating a strategy and sticking with it.

Bank loans and obligations, even if smaller in variety, trigger stress blood pressure and panic attacks. Maybe you are suffering from panic attacks and previously having dreams of flying bank claims all over you. These simple 5 measures will help you to get-out-of-debt if you find yourself in one of them.

Learn from Problems

Understand that learning from your mistakes manufactured in the past rather than to repeat them is a must if one wants to learn to escape debt, the best tactic one will discover. Considering you built a blunder is a vital step, although a brave. It's the beginning and enables you how to get out of debt as well as helps you to be cautious about other large or small troubles of your daily life.

Do your aftermaths

Like always, planning allows you getting out of debt and stays the key. Make a list of your everyday spending and view them.

Debt Snowball Effect

Debt effect is very detailed and straightforward approach to discover ways to escape debt as it simply begins in ascending order from smallest to greatest from listing all of your obligations. Subsequently to bring the minimum of the credit total be paid on the part of every debt, scheduling for future years, spending it down until the entire amount of the debt is settled and proceed this training till the finish of your every debt is paid from your number.

Be Productive

Being successful doesn't simply suggest reducing costs and reducing expenditure that is short in your whiskey, also, it comprises of carrying out work which generates cash that is quick to you. Washing your wealthy roommate's clothes, performing their type work with income as well as righting this sort of posts around the internet can earn a supplementary stack of revenue to you. Consider your internal potential, investigate it and only do it. You will quickly find a solution to how to get out of debt as well as the method of doing it.

Debt Reduction For Living Debt Free

Are you affected by carrying too much debt? You are not alone even as we are currently living in the world that encourages credit. A lot of people have the similar debt problem just like you. By ignoring it debt won't go away, you have to come up with a solution to eliminate it. There are numerous choices for you to revive your financial status and reside in the debt free zone. You could obtain a professional service that will help you or do it yourself.

If you are not in the toughest situation where bankruptcy could be the way out, you're able to execute a self-help debt reduction method to get your money back again and living debt-free. Here are the 4 suggestions to get you started:

Debt reduction via cutting costs

There are two sorts of the fixed, expenses and on demand expenditure. You may not manage to slice the fixed monthly bills like energy, gas, rental, mortgage payment, etc. But, expenditures like shows, activity, disco, a meal at the resort, etc.-can be reduced to save some money. The money saved can be utilized to pay for your debt. The more you pay the debt you owed, the faster it will be paid off and let you get yourself a debt free lifestyle when possible. In reality, the very first concept of debt reduction is always to remove bills that are recommended, and you should consider the motion to reduce whatever charges you can of maximum and income spend to a minimum the transaction toward the debt.

Stop buying on credit

Buying items with credit cards it's too easy-to-move out of control. People are inclined to not thinking when they don't use money as swiping the bank card is easy and so easy to buy things. That is why credit card debt will be the crucial aspect that causes the problem to many people. Consequently, the plastic cards should be removed in almost any self-help debt reduction program. Maintain one or two charge cards in the home for emergency uses, don't keep it anywhere which can be achieved easily. If different cards have balances, shift them for the cards which you intend to continue with, the remainder of cards must be finished since they put you of a risk of creating debt into your current balance

Get rid of the high-interest rate debt

In the priority list, bills using the largest sum and at the greatest interest should be in virtually any debt reduction software to be removed. There are numerous strategies to eliminate these high-interest rate scales. Among the popular alternatives are: balance transfer to charge cards that have low-interest rate; and you can also obtain a personal bank loan at a low-interest rate to clear off the debts that cost high-interest rate. The bottom line is, the reports with major bills and high-interest charges may snowball the debt quickly so that they must be eliminated first. That is one of the fastest options for one toward debt-free existence.

Find source of income

If you can earn more then you can pay off debt faster. There are various approaches to raising your monthly income. You could find part-time work making extra dollars for debt transaction. Besides the part-time occupation you might want to think about making money online. As many companies are online, nowadays the Internet is full of money, and they're trying to find brokers, better known as affiliates to promote services and their products. You'll earn commission on every sale you produce via the hyperlink that identifies you. It can be a real source of income for you. In fact, many online entrepreneurs are producing their living entirely from the internet. Thus, it is a proven source of revenue.

You have to locate a remedy to eliminate the debt issue if you'd like to call home in-debt free. You may usually start a self-help debt reduction program with the 4 tips above.

What Are Your Options

With all the existing economic situation, how to get out of debt can be a problem that lots of folks are wondering about. It is all too simple to get in a whole lot of debt before you realize it when up against complicated economic problems. Perhaps you had your hours of work reduced, had a medical problem that's set you back hundreds, or you have been let go from your work. Whatever the motive, you could have been required to begin living off credit cards or loans. And now you're in over your mind. How to proceed? How will you pay debt off since you're in so heavy?

You might have believed that things would return to normal quickly, and you would manage to pay off credit debt quickly. Often this is simply not the event. You may be having trouble finding another occupation or you've learned your hours have already been reducing entirely. Or maybe your credit card balances have gotten out of handle that even with a regular money you simply cannot make all the payments you must pay.

There are always a few things you can do to cover yourself from credit card debt. First off, you'll never get anywhere just by making the monthly premiums. You'll need to earn more money or at least increase the monthly obligations to begin lowering the balances. Most of the people, if they're serious about paying their debts off, can find parts inside their costs where they could cut back. Do you need to buy dinners at work every day? Can you go minus the lattes? There are plenty of luxuries that may be abandoned to free some funds to place toward your credit card debt up.

However, if this is impossible for you, there are numerous other activities you can do.

Negotiate Your Loans

Often, it is possible to negotiate less interest, or even a longer amortization period (the period of the loan.) This may lead to smaller funds that may be more feasible for you.

Talking with credit card company or your bank is clearly quite simple. Most banks and bank card companies will work with you to set up a fee schedule that works for you. Simply describe your situation in their mind and be honest by what you'll be able to and cannot do.

Debt Consolidation

Debt Consolidation is just ways to pay off obligations that are several with one huge mortgage using a low-interest rate. This takes care of the obligations much faster and typically reduces your monthly obligations. Also, it makes it easier for you since you simply have one transaction to worry about, rather than a lot of ones.

For this to function, you do not gather anymore debts and should incorporate all your debts. Essentially, you need to cut-up all of your cards and focus on spending off the complete consolidation loan.

Bankruptcy

Please consider bankruptcy simply like a final resort. If you have tried the three techniques above and you just can't get yourself out of your debt prison you're in, then you may need to consider bankruptcy. If you have the courts declare you are not able to pay your debts then bankruptcy might be the only option. You relinquish all of your resources along with the lenders need to take regardless of the court awards them.

Remember that you must hand over your assets not just cash. This could be your car, your property, savings, and other things of price. Also, you will not be able to get any credit for years in the future. No loans, mortgages or charge cards. This is a last resort if you are not able getting out of debt.

1. Pay Off your Biggest Debts First

Whether it is debt on student loans, mortgage, or credit cards, you may find yourself weighed down at some point in your life. Your debts may keep you working jobs you dislike just so you can pay them. If you want to stay away from financial problems, see to it that you pay off your debts, especially the huge ones. Do not let small debts accumulate because once they do, they may become bigger than what you expected. To pay off your debts, here are some pointers on how you can do that with the use of the Stack Method:

- Do not create new debt.

Oftentimes, people do not receive training in handling their finances and how they can live within their means. So if you are in debt, you are probably among them. You should realize that it is high time for you to change the way you live. You will not be able to get out of debt if you do not change your spending habits now. Learn to make a stand against marketers that try to offer easy money or take your money. You do not need to acquire more things to be happier. You need to have a financial peace of mind. You can achieve this by stopping your credit cards and making wise financial decisions.

- Rank your debts according to their interest rate.

Create a list of all your debts and their interest rates. Make sure to pay off your biggest debts first. Paying off debts with the highest interest rates is actually the key to the Stack Method. If you do this, you will be able to pay off all your debts more quickly. Keep in mind that banks and financial institutions can use interest rates against you. The longer you put off paying your debts, the higher their interest can be. For instance, if you own $10,000 in credit card debt and it has a 20% interest rate, it would take you nine years and eight months to pay off

$21,680 with an $11,680 interest if you pay the minimum of $200 per month.

• Lower your interest rates.

One way to lower your interest rates on your credit cards is to do a balance transfer. You have to move your credit cards to another bank. That other bank will then lower your interest rates. Make sure to shop around to know which banks offer the lowest interest rates with the longest duration. Do not forget to read their terms and conditions, so you do not get surprised by any changes.

• Come up with a strategic spending plan.

Get a piece of paper and list down your expenses and income tax. Be sure to include the minimum payments that you pay for your debts. Evaluate your expenses and rank them according to importance. Check which items are at the bottom part of your list and determine whether or not you would get rid of them. If they are not necessary and you can live a normal life without them, then do not hesitate to get rid of them.

Also, you have to know exactly how much you are willing to spend on different things. Set aside a specific amount for groceries, rent, dining out, clothes, etc. You have to discipline yourself as well. For instance, if you have already spent all the money you allocated for a certain thing, you should not use the money you set aside for another.

• Have a repayment schedule.

With the Stack Method, you need to cover your minimum payments on your debts first. Whenever you miss payments, your fees add up. Make sure to make the minimum payments on your high-interest debts. Your debt with the highest interest rate is your Target Debt. You need to use Stack Repayment as well as make minimum payments until you have finally paid off your debt in full. The fewer minimum payments you have to make, the bigger your Stack Repayment amount becomes.

• Reward your progress.

To see your progress, you have to track your Target Debt. Doing so will also allow you to see your milestones. Each time you make a progress, you should give yourself a reward. This way, you can stay inspired and motivated. You do not have to spend a lot of money on your rewards. If you insist on spending, however, make sure to get the money from an allocated budget. Refer to your Strategic Spending Plan.

- Compound your results.

When you have successfully paid off your Target Debt, celebrate. Congratulate yourself for doing a great job. Then, move your Stack Repayment to your next biggest debt. This debt becomes your new Target Debt. Repeat the steps that you did previously to pay off your first Target Debt.

- Be patient.

You may feel like you are being tested as you try your best to pay off all your debts. You may encounter situations wherein you have to shell out money that is not included in your plan. Whatever happens, you have to stay strong and patient. Do not be tempted to go back to your old spending habits.

Make Good Spending Choices

You need to be smart when it comes to managing your finances. You have to make good spending choices if you do not want to be in debt. There are actually lots of ways on how you can improve your financial status. You just have to develop more discipline and make certain lifestyle modifications.

For instance, you should plan your purchases in advance. Avoid making impulse decisions because that can significantly affect your expenses. List down the things that you need to buy before you even leave the house. You may also want to make a preliminary trip to the grocery store or mall. This way, you can check out the prices of goods before you actually start shopping.

Take note of their prices and compare them with their equivalents in other stores. Stay focused on the goods and their prices. When you get home, determine which items you have to purchase. By now, you should already have an idea on which items to get. When you are motivated to treat your purchases as important decisions, you can certainly make better spending choices.

Another way to avoid making impulse purchases is to avoid browsing store windows. If you see something that you like, you may be prompted to buy it even if you do not have any use for it yet. Likewise, refrain from shopping just for the fun of it. Once you buy one item, you will be tempted to buy another, and so on and so forth.

Refrain from making spending decisions when your judgment is impaired either. Sleep deprivation, alcohol, and drugs can all affect your ability to make sensible decisions. Loud music and hunger can have a negative impact on your decision-making as well.

When you shop, try to shop alone. If you bring a friend along, you may only be tempted to buy more. When your friend buys a shirt, you may also feel the need to buy one for yourself. Other people's opinions of your taste in clothing may also affect your spending decisions.

In addition, you should have self-discipline. Do not give in to the persistence of store employees. After all, it is their job to entice customers into making a purchase. This is especially true if they make money by commission.

Likewise, you should not allow yourself to be fooled by marketing tactics. External influences can be huge factors when it comes to your spending decisions. Do not purchase anything just because you saw it on television or a billboard ad.

Do not buy a product based on its packaging. The manufacturers may have included fancy terminologies or made various claims about the product. Do not give in to such claims. Use your common sense and figure out whether or not such claims are plausible.

Also, just because the item is on sale does not mean that you have to purchase it. Sales and coupons are great for things that you were actually planning to purchase. However, buying something just because you saw that it was 50% off is not ideal.

Do not forget to check the price tags. Beware of stores' pricing tricks. For example, if you see something marked $2.99, you may immediately think that it is just a couple of dollars. In reality, however, it is much closer to $3.

When you eventually buy something, try to pay in cash as much as possible. Avoid using debit and credit cards because doing so may only prompt you to buy more things. You should also not bring more money than necessary, and only withdraw money once a week. This way, you will be able to discipline yourself better.

Of course, you should also research about the thing that you are eyeing on. You can search the Internet for online reviews or read your local newspaper to check out consumer reports.

Furthermore know when you should invest in quality items or go to thrift stores. Sadly, a lot of people have this notion that an expensive price means high quality. Well, this is far from the truth. It may actually be foolish to purchase the most expensive brand for socks. After all, socks tend to wear out easily and quickly. Then again, you should invest in a good quality pair of shoes. Investing in sturdy and comfortable shoes is worth it since you do not have to replace it that often.

Try buying at thrift stores. You do not always have to wear brand new items. There are plenty of secondhand items that are still just as good as their brand new counterparts. Also, some thrift shops sell high quality items, so you should be able to find what you need for a fraction of the cost of brand new. These thrift shops are usually located in affluent neighborhoods.

Similarly, you may want to consider purchasing generic brands instead. Designer clothes are often expensive due to their name alone. If you are trying to save money, focus on the quality instead of the brand.

You'd be surprised to know that there are lots of inexpensive generic brands with good quality items.

When it comes to food, you should also learn ways on how to save money. For instance, you can buy food in bulk or shop for food during the time of day when they are offered at lower prices. You may also want to buy fruits and vegetables that are in season because they tend to be cheaper around this time.

To save money and to save your health, you may also want to forego compulsive habits, like smoking, gambling, or drinking. These habits are both bad for your body and your wallet. Getting rid of them will make you so much happier.

1. Build Wealth by Generating a Higher Monthly Income

When you are living from paycheck to paycheck without enough money to put into savings, then you need to make changes. If you have made the necessary lifestyle changes, including your spending habits without any positive result, then there is a problem with your income. It will be impossible to free up money if your income is just enough to cover your basic needs.

In such a situation, you need to look for ways to make more money. This is when the idea of passive income is critical. Passive income in its purest form is the idea of having your money work for you. This implies that you can make money while you are asleep. You perform an action once and keep receiving payment for that action over and over. Besides, you can have more than a single source, which you can refer to as multiple passive income streams.

The reason it is great to have a source of passive income is that it doesn't hinder you from working a regular full-time job. You can add the revenue from these two sources to increase your total monthly income. You still need to put in a certain amount of work to create a thriving source of passive income, but it doesn't compare to that of a full-time job in most cases.

You also eliminate your dependence on a single source of income when you establish a passive income source. To improve your financial security and rapidly attain a position where you can comfortably retire, passive income is vital. The chances of falling into debt become less likely with this option.

In the section that follows, you will find out some simple passive income ideas that you can adopt if you want to create more money to increase your savings.

Simple Ideas to Create Multiple Passive Income Streams

There are various forms of passive income ideas you can implement. Some require investing a certain amount of money, while others require a time investment. You will also find certain ideas that require both your money and time.

Here is a look at some of the passive income ideas that you should consider as your next source of steady income:

Stock Market Investment

Most people know about stocks and the stock market. It remains one of the most popular sources of passive income. It can be very profitable to invest in the stock market if you find the right stocks to invest in as well as the right online brokerage to work with.

There are numerous online brokerages available, so it is essential to do your research. When investing in the stock market, you should focus on dividend-paying stocks, which offer a steady income.

It is crucial that you increase your stock investments regularly to increase your dividends to a reasonable amount that can sustain your monthly expenses. Dividend refers to a portion of the profits a company pays to its investors. There are other options for stock investment besides dividend-stock investing, including stock trading. In this option, you buy stocks at a lower price to sell the shares at a higher price. You can also engage in short selling. These options require more time investment since you need to monitor the charts and do a lot of research.

Peer to Peer (P2P) Lending

Peer to peer lending refers to an activity in which you provide loans to borrowers on the platform. borrowers turn to these platforms for loans due to their inability to meet bank requirements. There are different online platforms on which you can register to begin earning returns on the loans you give out.

To ensure protection from a significant loss, you can share your investment funds among multiple borrowers. The interest on the loans makes P2P lending profitable.

Investing in Real Estate

There are several options available to anyone who invests in real estate. These options vary in the way they operate. Depending on your preference, you can choose from the following list of real estate investment options available:

- Real Estate Investment Trusts (REITs)
- Rental property
- House flipping
- Wholesaling of houses
- Vacation property
- Real estate ETFs
- Investing in real estate construction companies
- Real estate mutual funds

Selecting one of these options is an excellent way to gain passive income. Options like house flipping and wholesaling usually require a significant amount of time investment, so they may not be the best. The other options give you the freedom you need while you earn passive income.

Bank Investments

These are another popular passive income investment opportunity. Bank investments are easy to use and offer high security of your investment funds. Since it is a low-risk option, bank investments usually have a low yield.

When you decide to make a bank investment, you can choose to save money in a high-yield savings account, open a money market fund, or purchase a certificate of deposit. Purchasing a certificate of deposit is quite common, and you can create a CD ladder through this option.

When you purchase several certificates of deposits in increments, you are building a CD ladder. It is a straightforward option to engage in. Saving your money in a high-yield savings account offers higher returns than a regular savings account. It is common to find high-yield savings accounts mainly through online banks.

Making Money from Stock Photos

You visit a website or a blog and find photos that are so captivating and praise the owner for such a great image. However, not all website or blog owners are responsible for taking the photos on their sites. It's easier to purchase the images they need rather than investing in photography equipment and spending time taking the perfect image. They leave this task to others who have a passion for photography.

If you are one of these individuals, you can make a decent amount of money if you submit your photographs as stock images. Numerous sites offer this service, and they pay a fee if anyone decides to make use of the photo you upload.

Creating and Selling eBooks

The internet and advancements in technology have made it easy for anyone to become a writer. If you have information to share and you are sure people will need this information, then put it in an eBook. This only requires your time investment during the initial stages.

You can use self-publishing platforms like Amazon's Kindle Direct Publishing to easily share your book with your target audience.

Design a Course

There are several sites on which you can take a course online. You pick a course that has content that you think will be beneficial, pay for the course, and gain access to the materials, like videos. A site like Udemy is a popular platform for online courses.

These platforms require both the instructors and the consumers to run effectively. You can choose to become an instructor if you can create course content that you know people will want. You should have a lot of knowledge in the area in which you create the course and look for an excellent way to present it.

App Development

An idea is necessary to make money from app development. If you come up with a solution to a problem many individuals are facing, then you can sell your app on various platforms. You should understand how this works from the consumer viewpoint since you use a mobile phone and download some paid apps.

Blogging and Affiliate Marketing

Creating a blog can take up a bit of your time, but if you follow a proper schedule, you can balance running a blog with your regular job. A blog usually requires patience, as it can be a while before you start getting a reasonable amount of traffic. This is when it can finally become a source of passive income.

When you have a consistent amount of traffic, you can choose to run ads on your blog or website, such as Google Ads. You receive a commission on these ads following the guidelines that Google has set for its payment.

There is the option of affiliate marketing to make more money from your blog or website. This is an excellent alternative if you run a niche blog or site on which you talk about different products. You can add an affiliate link and earn a commission every time one of your readers purchase through this link.

License Your Music

You can make money off many things you are currently doing for free. If you enjoy making music during your free time, then you should turn this hobby into your passive income stream. People license their music to get a royalty anytime another individual uses the music. Many of your clients will be those who run YouTube channels, and your music may also feature in commercials.

Network Marketing

This is also popular as multi-level marketing. It may not be an option for everyone, but you can make excellent passive income if you understand how to make the most of network marketing. By creating a strong, large, and reliable team, you can earn a large amount of money as commission from the sales they make. The hard part is getting people who are going to match your effort to join. If the individuals under you are unable to invite others, this will limit how much you can earn.

Investing in a Business Venture

Investing as a silent partner in a business is another profitable method of earning passive income. You must be careful when choosing this option, as the high rewards also come with high risk. Unless the business goes public or is acquired in the future, you won't be able to enjoy the benefits of being an investor.

Spreading your investment across several companies is one way to minimize the risk of running into a loss. The option of investing in bonds is also available when you decide to invest in a business. Look for high-yield or junk bonds that will offer high returns.

Use Airbnb

For homeowners, renting out their place can be a good source of passive income. Airbnb creates a platform on which you can easily connect with individuals who need a place to stay. This is an excellent option because you are renting out what you already own. The only time you need to work is when you prepare the place for guests and clean the area once they take their leave.

Putting up Your Car for Rent

To save more money, you can decide to drive around less often. During these periods, your car sits idle in your garage. There is a better alternative. You can rent your car to individuals that need it. In addition to saving more money, you also earn more money. There are sites on which you can list your car, but it is vital to perform your research before choosing anyone.

Some sites offer a higher payment depending on the car you are renting out. You can also find a site that takes charge of the process once you rent it out. This eases the stress you might experience and makes it a dependable source of passive income.

Install Vending Machines

You can install vending machines in different locations to earn passive income. Purchase the machines and stock them with snacks and other items you are sure people will want to buy. You can focus on different locations in your town or spread your business to different towns.

It is not necessary to visit each machine every day. You can pick a day to visit once every two weeks to replenish the stock and take the cash from each machine. This is one of the few profitable businesses that you can run during your retirement

The Importance of Investing the Money You Don't Need

Most of the discussion in this book focuses on how to grow your savings. This is essential if you want to make meaningful financial progress. Nonetheless, it is also vital to put some of your savings into an investment. There are various reasons why you should consider investing, and here are some:

You Can Increase Your Money

The main reason people invest is to grow their money. Bonds, stocks, and certificates of deposit are some of the several investment instruments that can help grow your wealth. These instruments offer a return on your investments in the form of an interest or dividend payment.

The returns on the investments are much higher you can get when you keep money in a savings account. As the gains begin to accumulate, you will steadily build wealth through the money you invest.

Preparation for Retirement

When you are preparing for retirement, you are getting set for a period during which you will be unable to work to earn money. This means you need to save as much as you will need to cover your expenses. If you limit yourself to depending on the money you can save from your regular income, you may find it difficult to raise enough money for your retirement.

Investing makes it possible for you to earn a fortune. Start early and you can take more risks, which offers a higher reward. As you approach retirement age, you can reduce the risk you take on to ensure you don't lose the money in a bad investment. If you create a concrete investment plan, you can attain financial independence and retire very early.

Take Advantage of Employer-Matching Programs

Investing in a 401(k) is a smart way to secure your retirement and invest in your future. y Through active investment in your 401(k), you can qualify to receive funds from your employer, who may match what you invest in the program. There is a limit to how much your employee will match, but it is free money.

Lower Your Taxable Income

Investments usually help in reducing your taxable income. With a 401(k), you are putting money into the account from your pre-tax income. This means you are significantly reducing the income on which the tax applies.

Although it is not a situation you would prefer to be in, you can still use an investment loss to lower the taxable income on any profit from other investment options.

Attain Your Financial Goals Faster

When you set financial goals, there is a duration for achieving these goals. If your goal is to buy a house, you can make this goal faster if you decide to invest your money at a higher rate than keeping it in a savings account that offers a lower rate. Working towards a long-term goal like financing your children's college fees will be much easier if you invest your money early.

1. How Can You Be Financially Free and Debt Free

How Do I Achieve Financial Freedom

We all understand the feeling—the panic that sets into your stomach while you see the invoice for a sudden vehicle restore. How are we going to pay for that? However, what if a vehicle restore becomes just an inconvenience? Rather than traumatic, you pay the bill without wondering twice. Per week later, you've forgotten that it even passed off! That's how little it impacts your economic situation. It's now not an emergency. It's barely a hiccup!

Do you sense that sense of alleviation? That's what economic freedom appears.

Paying for a car restore without strain is just a small part of the photo. It's more than simply being able to manage to pay for emergencies. It understands you

don't ought to fear approximately retirement due to the fact you've labored with your economic guide to making investments consistently for many years. It's the liberty to stop your J-O-B from doing something you love, even supposing method getting paid less.

Economic freedom method that you get to make life choices without being overly pressured approximately the financial effect because you are prepared. You manipulate your finances instead of being managed by means of them.

The route to financial independence isn't a get-wealthy-short approach. And economic freedom doesn't suggest which you're "free" of the duty of coping with your money nicely—quite the alternative.

Having complete control over your price range is the fruit of tough paintings, sacrifice, and time. And all of that attempt is worth it!

What Does monetary Freedom suggest to You?

Monetary freedom has to be non-public. Dream massive and get particular approximately your purpose.

What does monetary independence appear like for you? Perhaps it appears something like this:

Freedom to pick a profession you adore without annoying approximate money

Freedom to take a global trip every yr without it straining in your budget

Freedom to pay cash for a brand new ski boat

Freedom to respond to the desires of others with outrageous generosity

Freedom to retire an entire decade early

When you are financially impartial, you have alternatives. You don't have to marvel in case your financial institution account can handle changing your hot water heater or buying groceries for a single mom who simply misplaced her process. See how ordinary human beings built notable wealth in my new book, ordinary Millionaires.

"whilst you are financially impartial, and you have got options. You don't marvel if your financial institution account can cope with replacing your hot water heater or buying groceries for a single mother who just misplaced her process." —Chris Hogan

That may sound too proper to be genuine, but you can try this! Right here's how to start your personal journey to financial freedom!

Step #1: discover ways to manage money

Your receiver's get ahead if you don't have a plan in your cash. Alternatively, you'll locate your self wondering wherein your cash went on the quit of every month! That's now not financial independence; that's a recipe for monetary disaster

Building wealth is impossible if you're living paycheck to paycheck. Provide each dollar a name before the month starts off evolved, and song your spending at some point of the month. If you continually overspend or below spend in positive regions, you may usually regulate the amount in each class.

"constructing wealth is impossible in case you're residing paycheck to paycheck. Provide every dollar a name before the month starts off evolved, and tune your spending at some stage in the month." —Chris Hogan

Budgeting is essential to get your budget at the proper tune; however, it doesn't quite there. Even after you reap financial freedom, you'll need nevertheless entire a completely unique price range each month. No matter how lots of cash you have, you need a plan.

Your receiver's get to financial independence on coincidence. Budgeting is step one for constructing wealth on purpose.

Step #2: easy Up Your price range

After you start learning the way to manipulate money, you may comprehend you've made some mistakes together with your budget in the beyond. That's k! However, in case you want to be financially impartial, you need to smooth up the mess earlier than you can begin constructing wealth.

This means if you have debt like credit score cards, student loans, or car loans, it's time to get extreme, approximately kicking it to the lower.

Why? Because while you owe cash, your paychecks have a person else's name on them. If you want to attain your intention, you need your full income at your disposal, no longer bits, and portions that can be left over after paying credit score card bills and student loan bills.

Paying off your debt helps you lay a basis to construct wealth on the way to last. Make certain you've got $1,000 saved earlier than you begin tackling your debt. You don't want a sudden cost to derail your development!

The majority sense like they got a raise once they start budgeting in order that's accurate information for you. Throw all of that greater at your smallest debt till it's long gone. Then hold the snowball rolling! Paying off debt is hard work; however, there's not anything like the sensation of really maintaining the cash you carry in every month!

When you're debt-unfastened, live there for precise. Having debt undermines your potential to construct wealth and puts your monetary plan in danger. It's simple. Steer clear of debt!

Step #3: Be clever about Your career choice

Your largest wealth-building device is your income. So in relation to deciding on a profession, there are loads of factors at stake. There's no purpose to live stuck at a lifeless-end job, especially if it's making you depressing. Finding a task that you revel in that also supports your dreams of monetary security will assist you to enjoy the journey.

So what have you looked for? Here are a few matters to keep in thoughts:

Where do you want to be in 10 years? Begin with the end in thoughts. Does this task make you feel along with your typical goals?

Is there a profits-earning capability? Even if you're not making your dream salary from the beginning, make sure there may be a possibility on your earnings to grow as your value will increase.

Are you able to grow? Are there opportunities so that it will flow up and grow in my opinion and professionally?

Do you revel in work? Don't spend a career at a process you hate. Find something you're captivated with that allows you to use your presents and abilities.

Do the advantages guide your dreams of economic freedom? Your alternatives for retirement financial savings and medical health insurance can dramatically affect your potential to build wealth.

Your choice of a profession can have a big effect on your lengthy-term economic plan, so take it critically!

Step #4: Create a strategy for brief-time period financial savings

Consider in case you had to pull money out of your 401(k) while your own home's A/C unit had to be replaced. What is the case did you need to open a credit card to pay for groceries after losing your task? How would you ever get beforehand if you kept borrowing money from your destiny? You wouldn't.

In case your goal is economic freedom, you need a buffer for the sudden existence occasions that appear to anybody, like vehicle upkeep, damaged home equipment, and medical deductibles. That's why you must increase your emergency fund to cowl 3 to 6 months of prices after you're out of debt.

Having the coins on hand to cowl an unexpected existence event gives you peace of thoughts and is a crucial part of your average financial plan. As soon as you have that absolutely funded savings account, you'll start to sense greater flexibility for your budget. You'll have the ability to say sure to purchasing splurges and forte lattes without guilt in any respect!

Since you're now not taking up debt, you'll also need a savings plan for huge purchases that aren't emergencies. Permit's take summer vacation as an example. It's easy! Create a line item on your monthly budget and divide the total amount with the aid of the months you need to shop. You're not living in debt anymore, and which means you can experience your holiday as an alternative to having a credit score card invoice follow you home.

With a complete emergency fund and a plan to cowl large purchases in location, you'll have a financial basis to begin making an investment.

Step #5: study Your funding options

Now that you have a plan for quick-time period savings, you're equipped to associate with a financial consultant who permits you to make the maximum of your long-time period investment alternatives. The coolest information is, the sooner you start investing, the greater the time your money has to develop. That's the power of compound interest at work. Right here's the way to get started out:

Retirement savings

Start through working with your financial guide to take benefit of the tax-desired retirement money owed, which are to be had to you at paintings, like your 401(ok) or 403(b). How an awful lot has to you, make investments toward retirement? Shoot for 15% of your income. And if your business enterprise gives an in shape on contributions for your 401(okay), take it! Don't say no to lose cash.

Why is a Roth a very good concept? When you invest in a Roth 401(ok) or Roth IRA, the money you invest grows tax-free. This means you don't ought to pay taxes on it when you withdraw cash in retirement. That's a massive gain you don't need to miss out on.

College financial savings

In case you're already contributing 15% of your earnings to retirement, and you want to start saving for your children's university fund, you may start by investing in an education savings account (ESA). Like a Roth IRA, the cash you make contributions to an ESA grows tax-free, which means that you gained pay taxes on it while it's used to cowl university costs. Presently you can make a contribution as much as $2,000 in step with 12 months for every baby in an ESA. Profits limits do observe, and your investing pro will let you recognize if the ones affect you.

In case you need to keep beyond an ESA, talk on your monetary guide approximately a 529 plan. Those plans also grow tax-loose! Simply be aware that there are a few 529 plans you have to avoid. Steer clear of pre-paid training plans and glued funding options.

The outstanding element approximately saving to your youngsters' university is that by assisting them keep away from pupil debt, you're placing them up for monetary freedom too!

Real-estate Investments

Your private home should be part of your plan for monetary freedom, not something conserving you again from accomplishing it. That's why it's so important to make smart decisions about the type of home you buy and how you pick out to finance it. If you buy a domestic that may be desirable funding, it will keep growing in cost because the years cross by using.

When you're investing 15% of your income into retirement money owed, you ought to use any extra cash coming in to repay your property. Attack it with a vengeance! Casting off your mortgage is a large milestone in your journey to financial independence.

Don't even consider owning condominium residences until your home is paid for. Or even then, you must best spend money on condominium houses if you could find the money for to pay coins for the belongings, and also you're inclined to deal with any hassle concerned in the condominium technique.

Taxable Investments

When your own home is paid for, you may contribute extra than 15% of your earnings to investments. However, before you leap to taxable making an investment, make certain you're taking advantage of all of the tax-desired debts you could—like your administrative center 401(ok) and IRAs.

In case you're prepared to move into taxable accounts, stick with an easy making an investment approach and paintings with your economical advisor to pick out an exact increase stock mutual budget with a protracted history of above-average overall performance.

When you invest outside of tax-preferred retirement accounts, you'll pay taxes at the money you make investments. You must additionally be prepared to pay taxes on capital gains and certified dividends. But deciding on mutual finances with a low turnover price will let you minimize the tax effect.

Step #6: Be active in your adventure to monetary Independence

Making the right funding selections is step one; however, staying in song with your fund performance is essential to getting the most out of your investments. Putting your investments on autopilot isn't a funding method.

But the concept of actively making selections about your investments may additionally feel overwhelming. If it feels that manner to you, you're now not by myself. According to a constancy, have a look at in their Net Benefits contributors, seventy-seven % of Do-It-your self investors stated they didn't have the time or investment knowledge to be assured in their investment choices.

You've labored hard to put the proper foundation, so don't leave this important step up to danger! You need the expertise of a monetary guide that will help you navigate your funding alternatives and courageous the USA and downs of the inventory market.

An economic advisor assists you in:

Make choices approximately your investment strategy

Rebalance your funds regularly so that you limit your threat

Create a realistic plan for what monetary independence looks like for you

Recognize what funding options you have past retirement bills

Installation a withdrawal plan for your specific state of affairs

With our SmartVestor software, you may find making investment specialists that will help you gain your monetary goals. Recall, the journey to economic independence is a marathon, not a dash. An expert economic consultant is a correct accomplice for the adventure.

1. How to Persevere When Things Get Rough

When you become comfortable with your budget, you might lose track of doing regular check-ins, then all of a sudden an unexpected curveball comes flying your way. All of a sudden you feel like you are right back where you started from. You instantly think that this entire budgeting nonsense is not meant to work out for you. Before you lose all hope in your ability to manage your money, remember, one financial hit or even ten does not mean you need to give up.

You started out on this path for a deeply rooted reason. Maybe it was to live debt-free, go back to school, start your own business, or buy your dream home, whatever the reason it is vital that you dig deep and bring that why to the forefront. When you get hit with a huge financial strain out of nowhere, it can be hard to put things into perspective and incredibly easy to get sucked into the overwhelm and dread.

The purpose of your budget, however, has been preparing you for these situations. While they may make a dent in your planning, they shouldn't completely derail your progress. Nevertheless, even if you have some of the expenses covered, it can be pretty discouraging to have to go back and seemingly start all over. Keeping your purpose in mind will allow you to not only overcome the financial setbacks but, it will allow you to rework your budget so you can get back on track and stay ahead of any other unforeseen money problems you may encounter.

Why You Started

When a huge hit comes to your budget it is important to look back on the list of things you will gain by persevering. When you first started out with your budget you should have made a list of how gaining control over your money would improve your overall quality of life.

If you haven't made this list, now is the time to do it. List the things you want to see change in your life when you gain control over your finances. The most common changes that can come about when you obtain the financial security you are after include:

- Feeling less stress
- Gaining more confidence
- Living debt free
- Obtaining the things that are important to you
- Setting bigger goals

Now, take a minute to really visualize this list coming to life. The financial goals you have set for yourself are what will get you to make this visualization a reality. How would sticking with your financial goals make you feel when you have accomplished the freedom you are seeking? This feeling is what will make it easier to overcome and twist and turns you may face along the way. Remember, a budget is flexible. When something major changes or happens in your life your budget can change to help you stay in control.

Financial Setbacks

What happens when you get hit with a setback that you did not plan or budget for? There is no way to avoid unexpected financial hits. Things will come up, medical bills, car repairs, new water heater, kids' activities and so on. These sudden financial strains can make you feel as though you will never get ahead or on track with your money management. Meanwhile, by sticking with a budget and setting aside emergency funds, these unfortunate expenses won't derail you.

We cannot properly plan for these setbacks. There is no way of knowing when life is going to hit you with an event that will require a great deal of money to fix or replace. As we have discussed, there are ways you can build up a small emergency fund to cover most of life's unexpected mishaps. The only way you can begin to build up these funds is to create the appropriate categories for them. This takes a great deal of self-control. When you notice you have a good amount of money just sitting around it can be incredibly tempting to make use of that money now. But, if you have been building upon your financial literacy and discipline, you know that leaving these emergency cash stashes alone will be an incredible lifesaver when something that would normally throw you off comes about.

How can you stay ahead or on track?

You should already have an emergency fund in place that can help cover some unexpected costs, yet remember an emergency fund is more for when you are not getting a guaranteed income. This is not a fund you want to tap into when you don't need to. Instead of relying on your emergency fund stash to cover unexpected costs, you can save a little for those unexpected,yet part-of-life events.

Setting up savings for the unexpected financial hits you know may eventually occur, will keep you on budget and actually keep you ahead with your goals. You know that car repairs are bound to come about, you know that there are certain things in your home that will eventually need to be upgraded, replaced, or repaired. You know that it is unlikely that you or your children will never get sick or hurt. By setting a small amount of money aside each month for these emergency situations you won't stress when they come about. No matter how inconvenient or unexpected they may appear to be.

You can create a separate fund for each of these instances and put away a small amount of money each month so that when the unexpected happens you already have it covered. Before you begin thinking you are already putting so much away for savings and now you will have even less to spend, rest assured a small amount like five or ten dollars a month or out of your paycheck will have little effect on you being able to enjoy your money. You are giving yourself the freedom of not stressing when you get a hard hit in life. You don't need to continuously place money into these funds. You can set a savings amount and once you reach that amount you can reallocate that money elsewhere. Maybe you only put $25 a month in your home repair funds until you reach a fixed amount. Maybe you set aside a few hundred for emergency medical bills. Maybe you decide to set aside just enough to cover half the cost of a major car repair. Setting aside even a little money now will keep you from being completely thrown off when an event does occur.

The fact is that unexpected financial hits may occur unexpectedly, but most are ones that we all experience. We just avoid preparing for them ahead of time. When you have a budget in place that can account for these unexpected hits, they won't feel like big blows to your savings when they occur.

Reworking Your Budget

Your budget is not a static plan. What may be working for you now, may not be ideal for you in the future. As we grow there will be other things that become important to us. Once you start seeing the success you have with sticking to a budget you might just find yourself believing that you can actually accomplish and have more of the things you only used to dream about.

Regardless of the reason, there will be times where it is absolutely necessary for you to review and rework your budget. But this isn't something you just want to do. If your current budget is working for you and nothing big is changing in your life in the near future, there is no legitimate reason to change what is working. If on the other hand, you are expecting a big change like a family addition, moving to a new home (either upsizing or downsizing) kids going away to college, or expected time off from work, you will want to revisit your budget and plan for these changes sooner rather than later.

Avoid the miscellaneous fund

You want to save up for those big financial hits but what about those sudden smaller ones that can end up adding up throughout the month? If you have children you know that there are often unexpected purchases that occur when one of them breaks something, spills something, or has an accident away from home. Or if you don't have kids and you suddenly find yourself in need of a new briefcase for work, running on your lunch break to buy a new button-up shirt because you spilled coffee on the one you are wearing but have an executive meeting you need to attend still. Or what if you simply lost your mascara, tore your contacts, or need to replace your to-go coffee cup? You don't want to just spend what you have if it is meant to be used elsewhere. These little unexpected expenses can cause you to panic and feel as though you have thrown off your entire plan. These little expenses can add up throughout the month.

One thing that most people do is set up a miscellaneous fund. This is often to account for the random unexpected expenses that may occur in the month. Having a fund like this in place so you can quickly buy new contacts when you accidentally lose one or buy a new pair of shoes when your heel breaks is great, but what often occurs is that this just becomes another shopping stash. Soon you are buying a new shirt, haircuts, a manicure, a second coffee trip, and whatever else you suddenly feel like you need. Instead of a miscellaneous fund, organize your expenses in their appropriate category. You can still have a little monthly emergency fund for when your kid decides to experiment on cutting their own hair or their sibling's hair, you can rest assured that you have some money set aside to cover this life's unexpected moments.

When Should You Change Your Budget?

For the first few months of sticking to a budget, you will want it to remain flexible. The first budget you create will most likely not be the one that works best for you. In the first month of your budget, you might realize you completely underestimated how much you would spend on food or gas and will need to increase those allowance. Other non-essentials where you may have overestimated your spending you might realize you can actually cut back on a great deal more. Once you have gone through the trial and error, your budget should then remain fairly similar month-to-month. And the changes you make will most likely be minor to help pay for short-term goals like a weekend getaway, birthday party, or family visit.

When a major life event occurs, however, your budget will need to be reworked. The most common big life events that will require you to revisit and make bigger adjustments to your budget include:

1. Getting married.

Getting married is one of those big milestones many get swept up in. Planning a wedding and paying for a wedding is a huge financial strain whether you are paying for the wedding or not. Young couples are especially vulnerable to getting caught up in planning their dream wedding where money is of no concern.

Even after the marriage, there are a number of other budgeting changes that you will now have to accommodate. Firstly, the budget you create is not just yours. You now have your spouse to consider. However, the way you decide to split up the monthly and yearly expenses is up to the two of you, but you will need to sit down and establish your financial goals together.

If you have been wanting to make a big career change and start your own business, you and your spouse need to come up with an appropriate budget that will allow for that to happen.

What about living arrangements? You may or may not have been sharing living spaces already with your spouse but is this just a temporary arrangement? Do you have plans to move into a bigger home? How will a move affect your commute? Will you need to shell out more for gas or will you be able to bike to work more often and save in that area? What will the new taxes look like?

Marriage is a beautiful new adventure and it is one you take with a loving partner. Most couples put off talking about their finances until it becomes a major issue in their marriage. One of the leading causes for divorce is due to financial strain. The sooner you and your partner sit down and discuss your finances openly and honestly, the better. If one of you has a substantial amount of debt before getting married, you might want to hold off on paying for a wedding until this debt is eliminated or at least at a more manageable amount. Many couples find that having a modest wedding better fits with their financial goals so they can more easily pass up the extra expenses that quickly add up to tens of thousands of dollars.

When you sit down to talk about a budget together you both should bring your goals to the table. This way you can create a budget that will allow both of you to work towards accomplishing what you truly want. This may not be a quick process, planning out the future of your lives together can take some time, but you can both begin to make the necessary changes or begin tracking your expenses so you can have a much clearer view of where you are at and the steps you need to take to get to where you both want to go.

1. Having a baby.

A baby is a wonderful life event but with the beauty of becoming a parent there comes a great deal more you need to plan and budget for. Will an additional family member mean you need to make a move into a newer home than you were actually planning for? Can you manage in a smaller space for the first few years? What about the necessities of clothing, diapers, wipes, formula, bottles, and the monthly doctor visits? Having a baby can quickly eat away a significant amount of your budget.

Once the necessities are taken care of you, also need to consider childcare. If you are married will one of the parents be staying home to take on the role of full-time caretaker or will you both need to be working? If you are both working how will you cover childcare costs?

If only one of you is working will that income alone be able to cover all the expenses each month?

There are a number of big items you will need to purchase for your little one as well. A crib, car seat, feeding chair, stroller, and of course items to keep the little one occupied can all cost hundreds of dollars. You'll need to work all these items into your budget before the baby arrives so that you can begin to make the necessary purchases, so you are ready to bring him or her home.

You'll need to do your research before making any purchases to ensure you are getting the best price for each item. You will also want to compare prices on the daily essentials like diapers and wipes so you can properly include these items into your essentials for your monthly expenses.

While having a baby is a joyous occasion to celebrate, understand that they can also bring a great deal of stress into your life if you do not begin to plan for their arrival now.

1. Change in income.

Whether you are making more or making less, any change in income will require you to rework your budget. Those who are blessed to be making more will rework their budget to help them reach their goals in a shorter amount of time. What one should be cautious of is falling into the thought process that having more money means you can spend more.

While you may be able to add to your fun money account you don't want to neglect adding to your savings and goals accounts. The easiest way to get off track when you are making more money is thinking you don't have to put as much importance on paying things the way you were when you had a lower income.

Those who are hit with an income cut will need to reevaluate what they are spending their money on. You will begin to find better ways to save with the non-essential items while still having the money to cover your obligations and find some fun.

1. Career change.

A career change can result in a number of changes that can affect your budget. Maybe there is a change in your income, you might have to travel further or less for work, you might be required to work longer hours or maybe you are working from home. There are many factors that can cause you to make adjustments to your budget. Some areas you might be able to cut back on and therefore put more towards your financial goals. Maybe you will need to add more to certain categories and therefore will need to cut back a little from your non-essentials.

1. Divorce.

It is unfortunate when you have to face a divorce, and the last thing you probably want to deal with on top of the other legal matters is your budget. Nevertheless, when you are going from either living off a two-income household to one, or you weren't working and now you will need to find work, your budget should be a top priority. Dealing with a divorce will add unexpected expenses such as lawyer cost and possibly other financial obligations that occur because of the separation. A divorce will cause you to completely restart on a budget of your own. You may have some of the same financial goals as you had when you were married but now you are going to have the satisfaction of reaching those goals on your own. A divorce can be a scary and unstable time financially, but it can also bring a whole new set of opportunities.

Budgeting Goals

Remember, the goal of a budget is to help you enjoy life more. While many of us run at the thought of adhering to a budget, the beauty of it is that you set the rules for your own budget. When you go through the process of truly uncovering what matters most to you, you won't shudder at the thought of a budget but instead, will look at it as another tool to get you to the life you want and deserve to be living.

Many of us tend to give up on a budget when we don't immediately see the rewards we want to be gaining. If you don't see the improvement you want, it is time to look over your budget again.

- Where is your money going?
- What changes can you make?
- Are you being honest?

Many times, a simple change in how you save your money can move you closer to your goals. For many of us having a separate bank account specifically for savings can keep us from unintentionally spending that money. If you notice you tend to dip into your savings with the idea of putting the money back in with your next paycheck, it might be time to set up a separate account.

A budget is meant to work for you. It is meant to help you bring to life your dreams. While you can't expect this to happen overnight, if you are not seeing progress then this calls for you to reevaluate your spending and savings. Are you truly using your money for the things that bring you ultimate joy or are you using it to just feel the instant gratification? Are you putting it away to be financially free or are you keeping yourself stuck by a limiting belief system and unclear values? There are a number of things that can affect your progress, and many can be easily changed but you need to be honest and have the discipline to make the changes if you truly want to gain control over your financial situation.

When a budget isn't working for you, sit down and go over all your goals again. Are they really what you want to achieve or are they things you think you need to achieve because your family is pressuring you or you feel like you are lacking because someone else has more? A budget is meant to cater to your life, and you get to determine how that life is lived.

1. Developing New Habits

"Chains of habit are too light to be felt until they are too heavy to be broken." Warren Buffett.

Let's explore some of the positive habits that you may already have or can develop when it comes to budgeting and finance. I'll start by emphasizing the benefits and importance of developing new habits as an attempt towards motivating you. I'll also talk about 12 new habits that you can start forming today that will help develop your financial muscles.

Starting off with the impact and importance of developing new habits which is very well captured in the quote above by Warren Buffett. When we fall into a financial pit, usually, it's not due to one or two days of overspending or money mistakes. It's because of the habits that have gotten us where we are. Habits have the power to put us on the top over a period of time, without really struggling or working too hard for it. It's the daily steps or small actions we take which form a massive achievement or success in the long run.

The best part is if the right habits are developed and practiced you don't even realize how long the journey of success has been. Take little steps each day towards a big goal and soon you've conquered what you thought was never possible. You'll be surprised that achieving your goals and dreams doesn't really take as long as you initially thought it would.

If you take action and implement nothing but the habits I've laid out in this chapter, your life can and will change in the following ways:

1. You'll be saved from the pains of being negligent and careless with money.
2. You'll never go astray towards the meaningless spending path.

3. You'll be relieved of being stuck in endless debt that seems to take forever to payoff.
4. You'll learn to be grateful for what you have (this is a life changing characteristic that most of us underestimate).

Moving forward and looking into the financial strengths, below are some of the habits that will surely help you get ahead with money provided that you implement them in your life. I've personally researched and practiced these in my personal life to get out of debt and bring security for myself and my family. Let's get to it:

· Pay yourself first – for every stream of income that you have (most people have one and that's usually their job) make sure that you set aside a portion of your paycheck for yourself. Before calculating your expenses, before paying anything, make it a habit to set aside a portion of your income for your future. Depending upon how much you make this could be 10%, 20% or 30%, but whatever it is develop the habit of setting this part of your income aside.

· Fix the Paycheck to Paycheck Cycle – we become so habitual to being in the rat race, that all the money earned in a given month is spent right away. Before you know it you're desperately waiting for the next paycheck to pay more expenses. It's easier said than done. However in order to get out of this habit, try some of these actions:

- Evaluate your monthly expenses. It may not be the most pleasing exercise to do, but once you do evaluate your expenses, you'll find lots of room for improvement. Cut back the expenses you don't need. Consider buying household items in bulk, cut down any memberships that you pay for but can do without, etc.

- Take a look at your bills, e.g. telephone, cell phone, electricity, water, fuel, etc. See what you could do to save on these. If you have credit card debt, can switching over to another card help you save on interest paid each month?
- Try to replace entertainment expenses with other activities that don't cost as much. For example, you like going out to dinners with friends, try developing another activity such as exercising or going for a run with your friend that is still enjoyable and costs you less. You could also cut down on your fuel expenses by carpooling.
- Try to use cash for your expenses rather than putting it on a credit card. Avoid getting into situations that you need to meet your month end expense needs by simply putting it on your credit cards.
- Learn skills that will help you save money. For example, consider looking into do-it-yourself manuals. Learn how to change your car engine oil. If you can fix things yourself you won't need to hire outside help to do it.

· These are some techniques, but the overall goal is to cut back on your expenses so that you have more room on your paycheck cycle and are not simply spending the entire thing each month.

· Evaluate the value when you buy something – to elaborate on this requires a bit of a mind shift. When we pay a price to buy something, we receive something for value in return. For example, if you've purchased this book, the content is the value that you receive in return. Now, evaluate how valuable this content is. Does it help you save more than the price for this book? It is something that you already knew, but now you will practice some of these habits? How much would those habits benefit you from a monetary standpoint, etc? It gives you a fair estimate in your mind on how valuable it is.

Let's take another example... going for a movie. When you do spend money on a movie, it's really entertainment that you get in return. After a few hours, once it's over the value diminishes. Don't get me wrong, I'm not saying not to spend any money on entertainment. I personally love going to the movies myself. But considering the long term goal and the value that a movie may bring to me, it's worth cutting back on.

Another example would be clothing. What's the value that designer clothes may have? Instead of something that looks just as good but is at a much more affordable price. Again, I'm not against spending on fine clothing, but if you're looking to get out of debt and become financially free it's worth paying attention to. Once you have achieved this, by all means feel free to explore your fashion and clothing desires.

· Make investing a part of your lifestyle – most people consider investing to be a complicated and difficult thing to do, but it really isn't. All it takes is a little bit of research and you can develop great investment steams. Become an "investor" rather than simply a "consumer".

If you're in your early 30s, I'd highly recommend that you make investing a top priority subject to learn about and start as soon as possible. There are thousands of resources available online, spend some time reading about them; find a role model or mentor that can guide you on investing and learn from them.

· Invest in your financial self – this is a wonderful piece of advice that can strengthen you for years to come. I cannot emphasize the importance of investing in yourself. Learning is part of growing. The more you grow mentally, intellectually and emotionally the more your life and financial wellbeing will increase. Make it a point to read a new book each month, or learn a new skill. Take a course and learn about communication, public speaking, negotiating, investing, finances, etc. There are countless topics to learn and grow from.

· Get rid of extra credit cards that you have and only keep one or two for emergencies. Credit cards are convenient sources of funding but also the most expensive. The more credit card debt you pile up and sustain over time, the more you'll be paying in interest in the long run. Now, they do become useful in certain situations and emergencies, but dropping the habit of using credit cards will save you more money than you can imagine in the long run. That's why I always recommend paying off your credit cards in full at the end of each month and trying to keep one or two only to help you in dire situations.

· Analyze your needs and wants and cut back but don't choke yourself. So our needs continue to be what is really important ... things that we cannot do without; i.e. the need for transportation, food, water, electricity, shelter, clothing, etc. Essentially things that allow us to live a comfortable and healthy lifestyle.

Conclusion

Debt can drive you into financial slavery by limiting your freedom and ability to enjoy life. We often find ourselves trapped in debt without even realizing how it happened. You simply take a small debt in confidence that you will pay it off in time, but before you pay it off, you take on another small debt. Before you know it, you are in huge debt and do not even know where to start to dig yourself out of it.

As you have learned from this book, there is always a price to pay for bad financial decisions. You may enjoy instant gratification from acquiring that designer watch, shoes, a new car, or the latest phone, but you will struggle in silence as you pay down the high-interest debt. As explained, there are sweeter fruits to enjoy in the future if you forego wants for needs now. For starters, you should forego some of those wants to pay off debt. Eventually, it will be easier to make sacrifices, save, and invest in wealth building ventures like real estate, bonds, stock markets, or entrepreneurship.

Above all, it is important to always work around a budget and be financially disciplined. You can be sure that it takes time and sacrifice to get out of debt. Moreover, the emotional and mental stress that comes from carrying a lot of debt is not worth experiencing. It is up to you to work towards securing your financial future and avoid falling back into debt. Start by building an emergency fund. You should have at least six months of your income before you venture into investments. Embrace goal-oriented saving in order to remain motivated and disciplined not to divert the money. Financial organization is key!

As you focus on taking out good debt to build your net worth and secure your financial future, it is also important to keep learning and researching new and profitable investment ideas. The economy changes daily, and that translates to new investment opportunities that you can cash in on. As the saying goes, the early bird catches the worm. Educate yourself on personal finance by reading finance books, following top-rated investors on social media, and when possible by attending personal finance and investment webinars. There is always something new to learn about personal finance, building wealth, and investments. Most importantly, associate with like-minded people who are focused on creating wealth and acquiring financial freedom; their spending habits are different and they will always have something new to offer.

Lastly, if you loved the content in this book and if it has been helpful to you, I would sincerely appreciate it if you would consider leaving a review for it.

www.ingramcontent.com/pod-product-compliance
Lightning Source LLC
LaVergne TN
LVHW090426210926
848480LV00002B/701
9798201582470